THE OUTRAGEOUS HERB LADY
How to Make a Mint
in Selling and Multi-Level Marketing

THE OUTRAGEOUS HERB LADY
How to Make a Mint
in Selling and Multi-Level Marketing

Venus Catherine Andrecht

Cover design by Summer Andrecht
Line drawings by Venus Andrecht

Ransom Hill Press
P.O. Box 325
Ramona, California
92065

SECOND EDITION

ISBN 0-941903-01-X
Library of Congress Catalog Number
82-060388

To constipated people everywhere.
May this book set you free.

This book has been written to inform and to educate. Included are suggestions of ways the reader can improve and maintain health. Anyone who uses this information without the supervision of his doctor does so at his own risk and cannot hold the author responsible.

This book is sold with the understanding that neither the author nor the publisher is offering medical advice. Self-treatment is hazardous. People who believe themselves to be seriously ill should consult a doctor of their choice for diagnosis and treatment.

WARNING

My intent was to write a true and factual book that would appeal to people who don't care a twit about herbs, their health or business. It's my way of gently educating regular people to a new — and better, I think — way of life. A sterile little treatise wouldn't do it. So, if you have any qualms about sex, please skip Henry and George. Otherwise, I think you're pretty safe.

FOREWORD

Dear Reader,

Having had 15 years experience in direct sales, I can appreciate what a tremendous sales aid *The Outrageous Herb Lady* can be to those of us facing the universal problem of building a successful business.

Venus entertains us with her story as she explains her struggles and how she overcame obstacles to build her own successful business from scratch.

As I read through the manuscript, I was delighted with her fresh, enthusiastic approach to recruiting new distributors, training them, and building them into managers. Her methods of finding and keeping customers are fascinating and helpful.

She has carefully interlaced her personal experiences among her sales tips, and she adds a flavor of humor as she explains such things as how to keep records, hold educational meetings and write a creative newsletter.

I feel it an honor to write the foreword to such an enlightening work, and I wish *The Outrageous Herb Lady* a world of success.

Herbally Yours,
Penny C. Royal

ACKNOWLEDGEMENT

One clear fall day I was at my mother's house. I was twirling nervously around the living room. My mother and I were discussing the thousands of books we'd read in our lifetimes, and how they were all starting to sound the same. I announced for the 50th time, "Mother, *I* could write a book! A lot of odd things have happened to me!" Mom agreed that yes, I surely could write a book.

I continued my agitated pacing around the room. Suddenly, mom said, "You're going to write that book. Why not? Sit down!" I sat. She slapped some writing paper on the table, sat down and commanded, "Start talking."

I did. I talked for six hours straight while mother wrote. Occasionally she'd try to sneak a break by trotting out to the garden or into her bedroom. I'd trail behind her, my words spewing out like rain on a roof. After six hours her hand stopped working, and I had to stop talking. But, we'd started something that *couldn't* be stopped.

Mother has since spent many days and weeks helping me put this book together. Once in a while as she labored over the index or the book's chronological order, she wondered if she had good sense in promoting this project, but she has certainly followed through.

This is a thank you to my mother, Margaret McWhorter, the green-eyed beautiful lady with the silver hair and the golden spirit.

TABLE OF CONTENTS

TABLE OF CONTENTS

INTRODUCTION

As I was growing up, my father would occasionally indulge in pulling a pair of tight infant rubber pants over his head. His forehead would roll close to his eyes and his ears would stick out the pant leg holes. He would then careen about the house in his jockey shorts, making odd hooting noises. Six little kids would scatter before him, shrieking with delight.

In later years, I recalled this fond memory in a college creative writing class. My paper was returned to me with a "D" and a terse note. The teacher had written, "Don't lie in my class. Write about things that really happen to you!"

Feeling deeply humiliated and misunderstood, I didn't write again for 20 years. My first attempt is this book. Naturally, I feel compelled to tell you that this IS a true story. All the people and events in this book ARE real. However, several names have been changed to protect those still in shock.

HENRY'S BALLS

I've been wondering if I should tell the truth about how I *really* got into herbs. I could tell you an angel left a package of them on my doorstep and I lived happily and well ever after, but that's not *quite* the truth. An angel did bring them, I think, but in a very unusual way. This particular angel was a man named Henry. He was about 65 years old, tall and thin, with an interesting Canadian accent.

My husband Keith and I met him and his wife, Clara, at a new church we attended one Sunday. After the service, the four of us and another couple went out to lunch. We were seated at a long table. Henry settled next to me. Keith was at the far end. I was busy tapping my silverware on the table when Henry leaned close to me and whispered, "You know, I used to have *turrible* trouble with my balls." My eyes widened. My mouth fell open.

Turning to face him, I whispered, "You did?" This was one of the most amazing and interesting things I'd ever heard. Henry stared at me intently. I checked him out, too, noting his polyester blue suit, flowered shirt and jaunty little cap with a small brown feather. This was going to be a fun conversation.

"Yes," he enthused. "For fifty years I suffered. I went everywhere — the Mayo Clinic, Scripps, all the doctors — no one could help me." He continued, listing all the places, all the problems. His voice grew louder and louder as he warmed to my rapt attention.

On the tale went ... 10 minutes, 15 minutes, 20 minutes. I never turned away or even fiddled with my napkin. This was some amazing story. At last, Henry built up to the punch line. "And then," he cried," slapping his hand on the table. "And then, my balls finally stopped working. You can *imagine* the social embarrassment!"

I certainly could! Turning to Keith, at the end of the table, I flapped my mouth and eyes rapidly in disbelief. He didn't notice. I turned back to Henry. Could there be more? What was the outcome? Sure enough, there was a happy ending.

"Then!" Henry was jubilant. "I met a wonderful woman." My eyes slipped to Clara. Did she know, or was she the one? Henry continued,

"This wonderful woman told me about the little herbs and they saved my life. Now, after fifty years, my bowel troubles are over!"

BOWELS, not BALLS. I laughed and stomped my feet. Henry laughed, too, delighted that I was so delighted by his miraculous healing. Dear Henry. His interesting Canadian accent had made bowels appear to be balls to my unsuspecting ears. If I hadn't misunderstood, I surely doubt that I would have followed the saga of Henry's bowel trouble with such steady attention and thus, perhaps, would have missed the ending, which was herbs. A beginning for me.

MY LIFE BEFORE

I remember lying in my baby buggy watching the blue sky move overhead. I remember being jounced along roads in Killeen, Texas. There was an odd ringing and scraping noise attached to these rides. My mother explained later that the rubber tires had worn off the wheels. My father was a soldier in World War II and we were *poor,* but I was happy.

A few years later, when we had moved to La Jolla, California, I can remember sitting on a small bank by the road, balancing on my haunches in a summer dress, a nickel clutched in my hand. I was waiting for the ice cream man. I was a happy, dumb kid.

My father and I spent a whole day, once, looking for the real Santa Claus. We finally found him. He was in the basement at Sears. He was settled behind stacks of brown luggage. My father was impressed. His little girl could sift through the thousands we'd seen and come up with the true Santa.

Everything changed when I turned eight. One of my sisters, Polly, got rheumatic fever. She was supposed to die. She didn't. She eventually recovered and now has a husband, two children and leads an interesting life like the rest of us. But we didn't know that then. We only knew that she might die. She spent a year in the hospital. Every night the whole family would get in the car and drive to the hospital. Over and back was 40 miles. I remember it well. The steep, scary, winding road. I would always lie on the floor so I couldn't see.

I have many memories of those days — the hospital itself, when we finally got there; the long, bleak halls; the medicine smells; people in white coats and pants striding down corridors; the cubicle-like rooms lined with stark metal beds; the coughing, spitting, vomiting; the moans and cries; the sight of dry, naked feet sticking out from under white sheets. I didn't like the place. I hated it! It smelled, actually reeked, of fear and despair. Night after night I'd pad along those halls. Eight years old and feeling 80. A surge of compassion filled me with the thought, "This is barbaric! Medicine is barbaric! There IS a better way. I know there is!"

During the same year my mother fell ill. She tried to hide it from us. She never complained. Sometimes I'd find her doubled up on the bed, holding the pain in her side. She was sick for seven or eight years, long after Polly had recovered. She saw countless doctors and had three major operations before the cause was found and remedied. She was born with too much bowel. Stress had caused it to spasm and lock. She barely lived through the last operation.

While my sister was still in the hospital and my mother was ill, my father's mother came to live with us. She was going to help us. She was going to relieve the burden. I found grandma pretty interesting. She used to chew up her food, then, taking it from her mouth, she would hand feed her two mean chihuahua dogs. These dogs wore hairy, red sweaters and showed their teeth a lot. At 70, grandma dyed her hair red. She would jump on the table and do the Wild Tahitian Hula. She also sang, "Sam, Sam, The Lavatory Man ...." But she would never tell me the ending. Grandma also spent many hours telling me how she was being raked up and eaten alive ... by cancer. These stories stopped — fast — when my mother overheard her. Grandma was bundled off to a new and a happier — for us — home.

You may wonder why I have slipped some of my past into this book. Each of us has a life story. It influences who we are and what choices we make in our lives. If I hadn't had this background, Henry's balls would only have amused me — not turned my life onto a new and sunlit path.

Sickness was all around me as a child. It affected me deeply. Eventually, it spilled forth into my physical body and I had a nervous breakdown. No one realized I had one, except me. I was constantly afraid. Afraid of long illnesses. Afraid I was going to die. If I stepped on a twig, I was sure I had blood poisoning. Every lump was cancer. All food was suspect; if I swallowed it I might choke to death. At eight years old, I had turned into a perfect ninny.

Worst of all, I knew it. Still I couldn't stop. Fear of disease had a heavy hold on me. If I did get sick, nothing, no one, could help me. Hadn't I seen and heard the results of traditional medicine? I was taken to a doctor who discovered a serious kidney infection. He gave me sulfa, and I promptly had a severe reaction. The doctor figured my kidney would clear up. As for my mental state? He advised my parents to cut a switch and blister my rear.

I found myself living in two worlds. One was the normal world. Going to school. Watching bugs in a rose bush. Reading books. The other was a place I lived in when fear took over.

I saw my options clearly. Overcome "it" or "it" would overcome me. I fought for myself for many years. With much emotional pain, I pulled myself up, repairing damage as it appeared. I thought I would never be healthy again. Up to age 33, I manifested a multitude of exotic symptoms and infirmities. Carted off to officeloads of doctors, I submitted my body to endless X-rays and scores of other inhuman and painful tests.

By the time I met the herbs, I was more or less adjusted to my life. Chronic exhaustion plagued me. The thought of a day at the fair would have me in tears. Every year in October, I got a sore throat that immediately went to my lungs. This would last until March. Two or three weeks at a time were spent in bed. My body often hemorrhaged. I had a long history of menstrual problems. Menstrual problems that made me wish for death, month after month, year after year. All the symptoms of a diaphragmatic hernia sat in my stomach. For two and a half years, I sapped what little energy I had, trying to get pregnant. I had one miscarriage before I had my one and only child. Then came a divorce and remarriage. Meanwhile, I worked steadily and tried to have a good time.

One day I said, "God, the doctors and drugs have had me for thirty-three years. I'm only worse. I have to find another way. I can't live like this. PLEASE help me." It was said with my heart and God heard me. He obviously knows my nature and sent Henry with his balls.

Please don't think that I want to totally do away with modern medicine. Without modern medicine, my mother and sister would be dead. Modern medicine is capable of heroic rescue methods when all else fails. But if you ask a doctor, a *good* doctor, about his lifesaving ability, he will say, "I don't heal. I put the body in the best condition for healing that I can, but the body heals itself." That puts the responsibility on us to keep our bodies in the best possible condition. We need to educate ourselves and all those we care about. We need to learn the simple methods of health care which will help our bodies help themselves. That's what Henry did for me. He showed me that I didn't have to depend on doctors to feel good.

WHAT ALLERGIES?

Henry invited me to a dessert party one night. An exotic herb lady was to be the main speaker. The topic was "Additives and Chemicals in our Foods." It also covered the overuse of X-rays, unnecessary operations and the general nutritional ignorance and rotten health enjoyed by the American public.

It frightened me. Like a sinner at confession, I whirled imaginary rosary beads. I ticked off all the ways I had abused my body: white flour; sugar; drugs; dead foods; packaged, canned, adulterated, colored, preserved foods; coffee; tea; hard liquor; smoking; X-rays. And the irreversible sin — I gave up my tonsils. What could save me from my past and present?

But there was hope. I heard how certain herbs, historically, flush the kidneys, liver and lungs. Other herbs, historically, clean the blood stream and the bowel. Still other herbs, historically, repair the body. I also learned to use the word *historically*.

No one claimed that herbs cure. That's illegal, as well as untrue. The herbs don't cure. The body cures. The herbs can provide the body with earth elements. The body takes what it needs and repairs itself. It all made sense, and I felt a strong inner confirmation. This was my answer.

Keith, also, found an answer. He had come to eat the desserts. But when he learned that 92 percent of all Americans supposedly have worms, he had an instant mental conversion. He bacame an herb believer that night and left the party with a bottle of black walnut hulls clutched to his breast.

Before the party was over, I lost all pretense at decorum. Hopping around the room, I asked questions. I begged people to tell me their personal herb stories. I was interrupted in my exciting quest by Henry taking his turn at the front of the room. Knowing what interesting information Henry could impart, I gave him my full attention. He began with the Herb Marketing Plan. He flashed huge charts with black numbers and stick figures. Steadily, he penciled in the mathematics of sharing herbs with friends and family. This was dull! He moved doggedly, vying for my attention. I didn't care! I had no interest in *selling* herbs; I just wanted to *take* them.

And take them I did! The first week I worked on $150 worth of herbs. Every few days I was back to Henry for another, and different, load. Sitting up nights, I read tons of herb books. Reading through reams of diseases, I would exult, "Hurrah! I have this one. And that one! Those symptoms and that problem fit me exactly."

It was one of the most exciting and fun times of my life. I raced through pages of herb books. I looked for more of my personal diseases. Matching them with various herbs and combinations was tremendous fun. How incredibly fortunate to have so much wrong with me. I was so grateful. I could try them all!

I did try them all. And got very sick. I remember lying in bed, at dusk, a victim of diarrhea and a heavy chest cold. My husband, Keith, peered down at me, his eyes like those of a chicken in the dark. "I thought those herbs were supposed to make you better, not worse," he said.

"Oh, they will!" I promised, "They will!"

I had hope. I had to have hope. I had nowhere else to turn. Only later did I learn what I had done to myself. I had used bags and bottles of herbs traditionally known as cleansers. (Traditionally is another safe word like historically.) I hadn't remembered about the builders. It only makes sense, "Don't cleanse more than you build." I did learn one thing from my amazing beginnings. It's hard to kill yourself with most herbs.

Headaches, diarrhea, even constipation are pretty common reactions. Colds and flu, too. Anything that can be considered the body's way of unloading whatever old stuff the herbs have stirred up.

Symptoms *can* be rather unique. One lady developed an incredibly itchy bottom. She couldn't go out in public for weeks.

In spite of my miserable condition, I was sure the herbs were going to work. Not only for me, but for my family. I dragged myself out of bed often enough to make sure everyone took their herbs, too.

When, at last, I raised myself from my bed, I realized miracles were taking place around me. Summer, my daughter, was seven years old at the time. She was chronically pale. Anemia caused deep circles under her eyes. She was skinny. Always tired. She was constipated and suffered from bronchitis. She worried me. When outright illness struck, I had every mother's nightmare. The little white coffin with flowers on top. Now before me was a beautiful child with a healthy flush across her cheeks. A child who begged to play longer with her friends. Summer had stopped coughing and started going to the bathroom.

It wasn't easy, mothers. Summer spent many evenings alone in the kitchen with a glass of orange juice full of herbs. If they weren't in orange juice, they were in honey, molasses, yogurt, jam or peanut butter. (Some mothers even resort to putting them up their children's rear ends. We never had to do that.) Bribery worked best. "Learn to swallow a pill and I'll give you a dollar." (Bribery has been used for worse reasons.) It worked. Summer was freed from the kitchen and released to a healthy life. Now, she rarely gets sick and is the fastest runner in her class.

Several years after we started the herbs, a neighbor came to me and said, "I can't believe it! What have you done with Summer. She used to be so skinny and pale and scraggly. Now she's *beautiful!* Her hair is gorgeous. Her skin is clear. Her color! I'm amazed!" I was amazed, too. That neighbor had never liked me. She had never even spoken to me before.

Another success story. As the months went by, I noticed a change in my husband. Keith's pot-belly went away. He lost 20 pounds. But what happened at the hairdresser's one day changed him forever. He went from a lukewarm herb man to very hot. His stylist pointed out an astounding fact. "Keith, what have you been doing? That bald spot on the back of your head has hair growing on it."

Keith's herb program got *very* serious after that. By the end of the year, he no longer displayed his life-long allergies. He spent a lot of time, during our marriage, telling me how bad his allergies were. How bad they had always been. He had stories of being unable to breathe. Of being very unhealthy and stuffed up. "I almost died as a child," he told me. "My folks had to get a very special German specialist to ream out my sinuses with an ice pick, and even that didn't help."

He impressed on me his need to have the window closed at night. It was a constant battle. I couldn't sleep unless the window was open. I had to have the window open to survive. He had to have it closed. If he woke up in the morning unable to breathe, his first greeting was "YOU left the window open!" If I had, I'd feel guilty. All day he'd cough and choke. When I hadn't left it open, I'd think he was nuts. Here was a man who spent most of each year trailing a roll of toilet paper from his back pocket (ready to catch his sinus drip). Hacking, snorting and blowing had been our house "Muzak." He constantly complained about how miserable he was. He blamed it on the cat, the trees, the air, the kids, me. He coughed and blew, snorted and swore. He was irritable, cranky and mean.

One day I stood at the window in the kitchen watching little brown birds. They hopped around outside, chirping to each other. Suddenly I realized it was SPRING and I heard *birds,* not Keith's nose. I ran around the house. All the toilet paper rolls were intact. There were no Kleenex trails from room to room. I found Keith in the yard. I stopped and took a good look at him. He seemed to be perfectly normal. He was sitting in a rocking chair, peacefully watching the weeds grow. "Keith," I said, "Look at you! You're not blowing your nose! There's no Kleenex all over the house. You don't have wads of toilet paper in all your pockets and up your nose. YOUR ALLERGIES ARE GONE! HURRAH! HURRAH!"

Keith looked at me, puzzled and disapproving. "What's the matter with you?" he said. "I never had allergies."

CONSTIPATED
CONNIE

Keith's dramatic improvement inspired me to spread the word about herbs. I was then working as a real estate salesperson. I worked in a large, fancy, very impressive office. Everyone, according to gender, wore beads, heels and ties. I was new in town and these folks were the only people I knew in the area. They needed to know about herbs. I'd start with them. Connie was my best pupil. Connie had a lot of brown hair. She was pudgy, had a bad complexion and was mean. She was also chronically constipated.

For some reason Connie had a lot of faith in me and seemed to think I knew what I was doing. She was a splendid audience and marveled at my graphic descriptions of intestines. "Do you know," I told her, "that when you die and they do an autopsy on you, they find anywhere from ten to sixty pounds of *old* fecal material in your bowel? And it's been there for years and years?"

I was passing on information from several fascinating books I'd been reading. Among them were *Childhood Diseases* by Dr. Christopher and *Tissue Cleaning Through Bowel Management* by Dr. Bernard Jensen. "Even if you've been having a bowel movement three times a day, like you're supposed to," I went on, noting the awe in her eyes at my revelations, "you might have only a channel left, just the size of a pencil, that the body wastes are passing through." We both gasped at the incredible thought and put our hands over our pot bellies. *Now* we knew why our abdomens were bloated.

I remember sitting at Connie's desk, in that very proper real estate office. I was penciling out a picture of what could be Connie's bowel loaded with pockets and strictures. Our eyes widened at the idea of all that packed fecal material. Both of us were surely loaded with worms, too. It was an incredible thought and it called for action.

I had access to a number of different herbal intestinal cleansers; *Prime Movers* that were supposed to be harmless and non habit-forming; herbs that historically and traditionally helped the bowel to heal itself, as the years of accumulated material slipped out. It was understood that this process could take a while. Even a year ... or two. So we didn't expect dramatic results.

We selected and used one highly recommended cleanser. Our abdomens swelled up like toads. We'd sit very stiffly at our desks. We'd bend, carefully and intently, and look over intricate maps, pictures of expensive houses and long-worded forms with our clients. We'd sit, looking dignified, while unusual and interesting noises pinged and whizzed from our bloated bellies. Our insides would rumble and pop and buzz.

Our clients would look, wonderingly. We'd look right back, the same expressions on our faces. What the heck was going on?

Once I even "tooted" twice in my chair. "Toot! Toot!" It sounded like it hit the wood at 50 miles an hour. To top it off, instead of unloading all the years of backed up garbage, we were *constipated!* Well, we had to fix that. I read and re-read all my herb books, until I figured I knew the problem.

The particular cleanser we were using was settling on the outer-most layer of the old bowel material. It was working on that outer layer. As we drank liquids, the top layer swelled as it prepared to ease off and come out. That *had* to be the answer. After all, we must have plenty of pockets of junk in there. The herbs were slowly and laboriously working through it. Connie and I had been chronic constipatics for years. That made sense.

According to the reading I'd been doing, some people were lucky and got diarrhea at first as a lot of poison came out. Time would take care of us and open things up. I expected to be swollen and gassy and even have some cramping for two or three weeks before my body adjusted. Connie wasn't quite as patient. She wanted some action. So I said, "Well, gee," as I flipped through my books, "would you like to take an enema?"

I had never taken an enema and neither had Connie. I had heard that some people got a real thrill from them, but I couldn't see it myself. I decided I'd have to be close to dead or crazy to take one.

Connie felt differently. I guess she was desperate, because she went home and took one. She called me later. "Venus," she cried, "I took an enema!" (She didn't sound relieved.) "I read the instructions very carefully," she continued. "I got the enema bag and filled it with water. I put in some garlic powder, just like the book suggested. Then, I laid down in the bathtub and let all that water run into me. I just laid there and let it soak in, like it was supposed to. It wasn't the most fun I've ever had, but it wasn't bad. But then the phone rang in the living room. I hopped out of the tub and raced to answer it."

"Oh, no, Connie," I gasped. "You didn't!"

"Yes," she said, "I never dreamed I shouldn't." She paused, then took a breath. "I sprayed every wall in my living room." Then there was silence. "Venus? ... I'm not constipated any more."

Connie's bowel experiences didn't end there. A few weeks later, at work, I noticed that she was always in the bathroom. *Always!* One afternoon she trotted into the office, very flustered. A pair of puzzled clients trailed behind her. "Venus," she whispered urgently, "We've got to do something. I was out showing property and I had to *stop at a stranger's house and use their bathroom!*"

I whispered, "Connie, what are you taking?"

As soon as we could decently get rid of her customers, Connie and I sat down and found our answer. Connie figured that one bowel cleanser worked so great, she might as well add the one that, historically, kills parasites, too. She'd been reading *Colon Cleanse* by Weiss and Burnett. And, then, heaven knows she wanted to lose weight, so why not add the cleanser that also traditionally eats fat as it cleans? And just to keep things moving, how about some cascara sagrada?

We learned an awful lot while we were together. We learned never to take too many cleansers and never to answer the telephone while taking an enema. Before we had finished experimenting with herbs, Connie's skin had cleared up and turned rosy. She had acquired a tiny waist, lost her cellulite (fat) and stopped being mean. To my sorrow, Connie moved to Kansas. It's been hard to find another friend as willing to let me experiment with them. I sure do miss her.

Life was becoming so interesting, and I was feeling so much better, that my real estate work started to slip. I seemed to be consumed, night and day, by the herbs. When I should have been going door-to-door, making cold calls, I wasn't. I was busy educating the sales people about the remarkable properties of herbs.

One day I had a new find: a mixture of herbs that were reputed to almost raise the dead. I thought it might do something for the office. Other people had told me it calmed them down, yet gave them incredible energy. I had noticed that it surely did that. I also heard that one person out of 25 seemed to go to sleep after taking it.

One day, I confidently held the bottle up to the sales force and intoned its virtues. I must have been convincing, because they were all practically pushing me off my desk chair to get some. We were all laughing and joking and having a wonderful time. Such a good time, in fact, that our broker eased out of his office to scatter the pileup.

He was a good-natured, middle-aged Italian with dark hair, kind of macho and old worldish. His words slid out softly, "What have you got there?"

I held up the bottle as if it were Ridley's Snake Oil and shouted out its virtues, "Thought to produce a sense of calm! Gives you so much energy you think there's something wrong with you! Take it too late in the day and you'll dance all night."

"Hey," he said, "give me a couple." I did. We all sat down and waited.

About 20 minutes later, Jenny spoke. She sat behind me and had been sniffling back a cold all day. "Wow! I feel good! I really do. I was going right home after work, but I feel so great! I think I'll stay and make cold calls all evening!"

I started clapping and hurrahing. I *loved* to see the herbs work. Suddenly, Darlene, forty-ish with long blonde hair and disco-type inclinations, leaped from her desk. She popped into the aisle where she started kicking and jumping. "I'm going out tonight! Oh, boy, do I feel good! I'm going to dance all night. This is soooooo neat!"

More herb approval. I loved it. The herbs were winning them over. I gazed around the room. Glen had taken some of the herbs, too. He was a good-looking kid in his early twenties. He always wore a suit and fastidiously combed his hair. He was very proper, clean-cut and hard working. I watched his profile as he stared silently ahead. Then, incredibly, he whirled into action. He slammed the lid on his desk-top brief case. Bang! Snap! Snap! It locked. Everyone was startled and riveted themselves in his direction. His right arm quickly curved out and swept the papers on his desk into an open top drawer. Slap! The drawer banged shut. Glen shot from his chair like a wild ping-pong ball. He snatched up his briefcase and was gone.

We all looked at each other in amazement. This stuff really worked. Even I was impressed. I glanced toward the broker's office. His room was totally enclosed by glass. You could watch him and he could watch you. He sat, facing us, behind a large oak desk. He worked elbows deep in legal pamphlets, books, phones and important papers. I noticed that everyone surreptitiously watched him, not wanting to miss the action when he turned on.

As it turned out, we didn't miss anything. He did. One minute the man was perfectly normal, busily writing , tapping his pencil, sliding papers around and looking hassled. Then slowly, almost inperceptibly, his elbows slid out from under him, until his forearms were flat on his papers. Inch by inch, his head dropped forward, finally reaching and resting on his hands.

The office became silent. Twenty-five sales people sat in quiet wonder. From the open door of the boss's office came a musical snoring, with occasional snortings and sleepy, slobbering sounds. We were impressed. He slept solidly. Probably the best sleep that man had ever had. At the end of a very quiet hour, he suddenly jerked himself up from his desk, looking surprised and bewildered. He immediately commenced writing and shuffling his books. We all looked the other way and pretended we never saw a thing. He was the one person in 25.

That was the turning point. I decided right there that my real estate career was over.

ASK ME ABOUT HERBS?

"You're a fool! Why did you leave real estate for herbs? You were making *big* commissions and you left it all to make nickels and dimes!"

I got a lot of supportive comments like that. Mainly from friends, parents, sisters, brothers — you know — family. The ones you always count on to straighten you out if you start to lean a little bit off your twicket. And would they take herbs? Are you kidding? They knew me better than to think I knew anything. You'll probably find it's the same with your family and friends. If you can sell THEM, you can sell anyone.

One relative, in particular, spent (and still spends) a lot of time warning me that I'd be thrown in jail. Sued. Locked up. How he worried about me. What was I "prescribing" now? "Watch it! Don't diagnose, I'm so worried about you."

I'd sing (and still do) my litany. "I'm not a doctor. I don't diagnose or prescribe. I'm an herb seller, and *that's all I want to be.*"

Others made fun of me. They called me crazy, knew I'd fail. They all made me plenty mad and often frightened and upset. One day, I just sat down with myself and said, "Okay, I want to sell herbs. I want to educate people about herbs. I don't want to play doctor or harm people in any way. I want people to start thinking for themselves and to realize they have choices about their health. If I don't do it, who will? I *know* I'm doing the right thing."

I made a solemn commitment to help and to educate. From then on, when I was criticized, jeered at or someone tried to scare me out of herb work, I simply wouldn't hear it. I had made my decision to sell herbs and to educate, and *that was that!*

If you wish to be successful in the herb business or any business, I suggest you make a similar commitment and set your goals now. Then let nothing deter you.

All those well-meaning friends and relatives were right about one thing, though, I was a terrific real estate salesperson. I did make big commissions. Do you want to know why? I believed in real estate. I thought it was the best investment around. I set out, enthusiastically, to make all my friends and potential friends (everyone I met) rich. I loved real estate and constantly studied and worked to improve my ability to help my friends and my clients. But *now* I had found something that was even more important to me than real estate. Helping my friends get rich paled in importance when I compared it to showing my friends the way to glowing health. But nothing was lost. I took all that I had learned about selling real estate and used it in my new business of selling herbs.

People ask me, "How did you get started? I can't seem to sell herbs! What's your secret?" It helps to have a background in selling, of course, but we're all natural salespeople when we get excited about something.

I tell them, "Here's exactly what I did. I was so excited about the herbs that I would talk to *anyone* about them."

When I was in real estate, we all wore little name tags with our name and the company we worked for. Everyone is interested and curious about real estate. People would see the name tag and ask questions.

"Have a button made," I tell them. "Have it say, "WE HAVE HERBS FOR THAT" or "ASK ME ABOUT HERBS." Then wear it to the supermarket. Someone will usually ask. Just be prepared to talk.

One of my distributors, Ann, decided to treat her gums and teeth with black walnut powder. She smeared the gritty black herbs all over the inside of her mouth. She was very careful to thickly cover the entire inside of her mouth, then squished it through her teeth for good measure. She hopped quickly into her car and dashed to the grocery store. She ran in, just to grab a loaf of bread.

Unfortunately for her, a lady stopped her in the aisle. "Well, what *about* herbs?" she challenged. Ann looked at her blankly, then remembered she was wearing her herb button that instructed, Ask me about herbs. Ann said she sagged against the canned goods and mentally beat herself for not taking off that button. She realized she was stuck and went into a fast spiel, trying desperately to keep her lips together.

I can imagine that lady, curiously watching the blonde-haired girl with the black lips, teeth and tongue. According to Ann, not only was she trying to talk sense through closed lips, she was also drooling black juice down her chin.

What if you're wearing your herb button, your teeth are clean, you're prepared and no one asks? Well, don't be shy. You can never afford to be shy in selling. If you notice someone glancing at your button, smile and ask if they're curious. If you get any response at all to that question, immediately answer their questions and launch into your own amazing and amusing herb results.

Have some cards made up with your name, phone number and the company you work for printed on them. "If you can't afford cards," I tell them, "make some. Then, hand them out. Try to see how fast you can get rid of them."

You may get some rebuffs, but you can't let that bother you. Most people are nice and all of them are interesting. You'll find picking up people in supermarkets a lot more entertaining and profitable than going to a bar.

For example: I run to the store to get a few things for dinner. Over in the produce section is a sallow-faced, fat lady. I can just tell she needs my help. I walk over near her with my herb button showing, a friendly look on my face. Even though I'm anxious to help this lady, I can't say, "Pardon me, but you look awfully fat and constipated. I'd like to tell you something that may make you look nominally attractive again." I can't say that. It's not only rude, it's illegal. My heart might be in the right place but my brain wouldn't.

She's looking at the cabbages, so in a nice neighborly way I pick up one. In order to make conversation, I say something like this, "These cabbages sure are small." She merely nods her head, engrossed in what she's doing. I'll have to think of something else to say.

Making every attempt to seem non-threatening and sweet, I stand there smiling and rolling a cabbage from hand to hand. I try to put myself in her shoes. What is she doing here? The same thing I am. "It sure is hard to think of something different for dinner every night," I say.

She turns to me, a loose bobby pin dangling from her hair. "It sure is. The same old peas, potatoes and celery ... God luv 'um, if I bring home something different, my family won't eat it," she says.

I've got her attention. Now, how do I get to the herbs? I have a few herb ideas I keep for such occasions. "Let me tell you how I make those same old vegetables more interesting," I offer. "I use a few herbs. Have you ever tried rosemary on your cabbage?"

She glances at me as if to say, "Who's Rosemary?"

"It not only adds flavor," I nod, "It's also traditionally used for migraine headaches."

"It is?" she says, "Well, I sure have those. I've got hot flashes, too." She now turns to me in earnest. "The migraines I've had for twenty-five years. And my heart jerks. Nothing sits well on my stomach. My ankles crack."

"Have you been to a doctor?" I ask. (She may be too big a problem for me, in more ways than one.)

"Oh, my, yes," she exclaims. "Countless doctors. They've all given up on me. One of them even had the gall to tell me a good physic might help."

I cluck sympathetically. This is getting more interesting. I give her my entire attention. When she sees how interested I am, she really warms to her subject. Her family has stopped listening to her miseries years ago, and here I am, a total stranger, obviously enthralled. She goes on listing and elaborating on her problems.

When I, literally, can't bear to hear any more, I ask again, "Are you sure your doctor knows about all this?" She reassures me that he does and isn't the least bit interested. "There are a lot of historically used herbs that might help you. I've got lots of books on the subject. I'd be glad to share some information with you." I hand her my card. "Give me a call. I'll look up some herbs that are traditionally used for your problems."

She takes my card and looks at it like it's a map of another planet. "You mean," she says, "you mean I can just sprinkle a few herbs on my vegetables and I'll feel better?"

"Not exactly," I laugh, "You'll need a bit more than that. But I know an herb lady and can get them for you in capsules." Suddenly, I have a bright idea. "Give me your name and phone number, in case you loose my card."

Later that evening, I call her. "This is Venus, the herb lady. I met you over the cabbages ...." I always identify myself. I never assume someone will remember me. We chat a while about herbs and their uses. I liberally sprinkle our conversation with instances when the herbs have helped me. I also throw in a few true stories about why my herbs are superior to ones she can get off the local shelves. If I don't, the second I hang up, my cabbage lady will be off the phone and running to her nearest health food store. I say this, because at this point in our conversation, my lady is breathing with happy excitement over the phone. "What do these herbs cost?" she asks.

I tell her the cost of each herb individually. "Well, hawthorn runs $6.95 per bottle. The building combo is $8.20 ... and there's one hundred capsules in each bottle. Actually, you'll get two or three capsules extra! And the dandelion is $5.50 ... plus there's a little tax on that."

I'm careful not to add up the whole bill and announce, "Well, sure, that'll be $156.95."

My new friend might yell, "My gawd! I could never hide that from Harry!" and I've lost her.

By the time I've explained the herbs, how they work and what they've done for me and my friends, my lady is trilling with anticipation. She ends up by thanking me profusely for coming into her life, swearing that God Himself must have sent me and the herbs. I close the sale. "Okay, you want the hawthorn and the dandelion. And the building combo, right? Yes, that's $8.20. Can you pick this up tomorrow or would Tuesday be better?" It's simple. She's happy, you're happy and you've educated someone. Plus, you have a new, and probably devoted, customer.

15

MORE SALES TIPS

Here are a few ideas that might help you with your sales. When you ask someone for their name and phone number, say, "Give me your name and phone number." Not, "May I have ..." Saying "May I please" gives them time to look at you and think, "Gee. Should I? She could be a nut."

Identify yourself when you call or see someone. Never assume anyone is going to remember you. You may not be as stunning as you think. Don't take it personally if someone won't buy from you. Or listen to you. When people say "no" to me, I just think, "I did my best. I put it out there." I always feel sorry for them if they pass up the opportunity for trying herbs, but I understand. They just can't hear it ... yet.

When you get some interest, follow it up. Don't wait for them to call you. They probably won't. They get home and think about it or someone makes fun of herbs ... and they forget you. Call them.

When you get an order, name the time and place for it to be picked up. I used to deliver. You may want to do that at first. But I stopped that when my business got too big. I just started telling people to come to my house. "Can you pick them up from me tomorrow at three or would four be better?" No one has ever refused.

There are general directions on the bottles of herbs, but people will ask you how many they should take. You can't tell them. Everyone is different and has to work out their own program. Some people are like horses and can take incredible amounts and feel wonderful. Others are like sensitive flowers and can take only small amounts.

Remembering my experiences and Connie's, I always start my new herb programs *very* slowly. Herbs are food. Some people have a low tolerance for certain foods. I've made up a flyer that I give out with my herbs with suggestions and warnings of what to expect.

Be sure to give people your phone number so they can call you. Better yet, put your address and phone number on stickers and stick the stickers on the bottles.

As soon as I sell a new person, I make a three-by-five card on them. I write down the date, their name, phone number, address and what herbs they bought. I also make sure to put down identifying characteristics, so out of all the hundreds of people I see, I can remember them.

For example:

```
BROWN, MARCELLA                    Sept. 8, 1982
1115 Rose St.
New Town, Calif. 90300
Ph. (714)745-2001
Red nose. Wore lots of beads. Brought her little boy.
Found a plastic bag in the fish bowl after he left;
several fish in it.
```

You see? I'll never forget Marcella. When she calls, I flip out her card, quick as a whistle, and say, "Oh, hi, Marcella. How's your little boy?" People are very impressed by this. You've remembered them.

I also make every effort to recognize people by their voices on the telephone. They love that. It's hard on me, though. Everyone expects me to know them, instantly, and they don't give names. I don't like to hurt feelings and will sometimes spend half a day puzzling, "Who *was* that person?" Of course, it's a lot smarter to just ask, "Who are you?"

After you've written your cards, file them alphabetically. ONE WEEK after the sale, call your customers. "Hi! It's Venus. Your Herb Lady. How are you and the herbs doing?" People are very impressed that you cared enough to call. But, be ready for some interesting answers to your questions! After you ask how they're doing, you may hear, "Oh, I quit taking those herbs. They made me sick. They gave me diarrhea." Or, "They made me constipated." Or, "Mean" or "Tired" or "I got pimples all over my butt" or "What's the matter! My stool is blue and *explodes* when it hits the toilet. Should it do that?"

Most of the time, all of this is just wonderful. Tell them so. I get extremely happy for them when I hear how bad they feel. I tell them how marvelous for them that they're feeling rotten. I impress on them that they may be just loaded with toxins and they have to come out. If you are using cleansing herbs, they *will* come out. By the end of our conversation, the "victim" is feeling pretty happy about the whole experience.

It's rare for someone to have a real problem with the herbs we handle. We don't stock dangerous ones. Herbs are concentrated foods, remember? It's possible, if you have allergies to certain foods or plants, that you may have a similar reaction to one of the herbs. Be aware of this possibility.

Some folks get gassy or uncomfortable. I would simply cut back on the amount of herbs I was taking if that happened to me. I wouldn't stop, totally. I've noticed that stopping, for me, seems to negate the good effects I've had to that point.

Some folks complain because they don't feel bad when they're taking cleansing herbs. I assure them they don't *have* to feel bad. When I call other people, they may say, "Oh, I forgot to take those things," or they say they feel nothing. They don't "feel a darn bit different." That's okay. They haven't been on the herbs long enough. A good herbalist will say, "Give the herbs six months before you decide if you like them or not. Give them a real chance." Everyone is different in the way their bodies react to input.

Another group of people will call *me* before I can get to them. "I feel better than I ever have in my whole life! I'm calmer; I have more energy; I'm sexier; my cold feet have turned warm; I'm losing weight' my wrinkles are going away; etc."

I get so excited that I immediately start taking whatever they're taking. One lady swore to me that while using a traditional anti-aging formula her "skin had gotten smooth as silk, it's so moist, and my wrinkles are leaving!" She sold *me*. Right there, I grabbed that bottle and started taking the formula three times a day. By the end of a month, I noticed my breasts were almost double their normal size. It felt like someone was inside me blowing up balloons. I could actually feel myself growing.

Each day I thought, "One more shot of energy into this area and I'm going to explode!" I was actually afraid I wouldn't stop expanding. My husband was, of course, overwhelmed by the action taking place. However, I finally decided I did *not* like an enormous bust and discontinued the magic elixir. But, I sure was impressed!

After the *one-week* checkup on clients, I wait a *month,* then call again: "How are you and the herbs doing now?" I'm concerned and very curious. I really want to know.

Most of them say, "I can truly feel a difference. They're certainly working." Also here's where you may hear the most fascinating happenings. I've heard some real stunners.

First, there was George. George came hot-footing over to buy some herbs one day. I'd never seen the man before. He was 60, a wispy little guy with hairy ears. He plunked himself right down on my kitchen chair and watched as I soaped my dishes. "I want," he announced, "some of this here genesee. A guy at work says this here genesee really does good."

I eyed him. "Ginseng," I stated. "You must mean ginseng."

George was a restless, nervous kind of guy, but very intent. He persisted. "I want some genesee. Max said it worked swell for him. Got his pecker right up."

"Ginseng," I repeated. "It has a reputation ah ... for ... that." I was trying to be very cool and unembarrassed. George certainly wasn't shy, so I'd match him.

"Well," he went on, "I want some. You know, darlin', I haven't been able to get it up for 20 years. I did some quick numbers in my head. Since he was 40? Poor guy. "My poor wife," he continued, "she's been real good about it. But, it's hard on all my girlfriends. Every year I take a separate vacation from the wife. I go to Las Vegas. Got a lot of girlfriends there." He leaned back in his chair, expanding his scrawny, T-shirted chest. "Yep," he continued, "I'm having my vacation soon and I want some of this here genesee."

I was really enjoying this man. Even Henry couldn't top this one. I looked him straight in the eye. "Do you have any other problems?" I asked.

"Yep, I got hemorrhoids. Biggest ones you ever seen. They hang way down this far," he said, measuring about four inches between his palms. I was amazed. "And," he went on, "they're so damn long, they slap against my legs when I walk!"

He jumped off his chair. "No!" I shouted, "I don't want to see them! SIT! Sit down, please."

George lowered himself into his seat. (I wondered if it hurt.) "I want," he repeated, "some genesee."

"Okay," I said, "you got it. Come on."

He trailed me to my herb room. He was amazed by all the bottles and books and even more impressed that I ran the business, virtually alone. At that time, my husband traveled extensively with his job, and I rarely saw him. "What about you?" George asked, "don't it bother you to have no man around?" I assured him that I was all right.

George got his "genesee' and several other herbs, besides. He'd decided he might as well work on his hemorrhoids, too. Before he left, I explained things carefully to him ... about 15 times. "George," I said, "I don't know if you'll get over your problems right away. Have you seen a doctor?"

"Yep," he answered, "nothing wrong with my pecker. Just can't get it up. Just lays there like a dead worm."

"Oh, well ...," I ventured, "I can't promise you results. Herbs are a food. They give the body elements that it may lack and it heals itself. And, George, you certainly can't expect instant results. It could take months. In fact, I'd take the herbs six months before I decided one way or the other. George?"

I knew he wasn't hearing me. He had his mind made up that this here genesee was a wonder worker and it was going to do it! Especially since he had a handful of other herbs with a powerful and similar reputation. "George," I tried, again, "I can't promise you results. These are a *food*, George. Not a magic brew."

George clutched his precious herb bag to him. "Honey, this here genesee worked for Max the first night."

"George, it doesn't work like that," I sighed.

"Honey," George looked at me speculatively, "how do you get along without a man? You're a real pretty girl!"

I took a step toward the stairs and led George down. As I opened the door, I reminded him, "Now, you call me and let me know how you're doing."

He did. The next morning at 7 a.m. "Venus? This here genesee? It didn't work."

I heard from George frequently over the next month. I got to know about his "problem" in all its glory. I learned he was a handyman who tried to fix more than women's stoves and refrigerators. I heard all about the ladies in lacy see-through nighties and housedresses with no underwear. About how "it" still wasn't working.

One day he called to tell me that his hemorrhoids had slam, whooshed right up his rear and hadn't bothered him since. But, that genesee sure wasn't working and wasn't I lonely? He'd sure like to come over and give me a big kiss. I was always too busy.

I didn't hear from him for several months after that. I guessed he'd given up on the herbs. (Many people do.) Then, one day, he was on my doorstep, crowing. "Venus, honey, I'm a new man. That stuff sure is swell. I drive down the street and see all those pretty girls and my pecker rides straight up all the way. I've had wet dreams every night," he chortled.

I winced. George had always been very graphic. "And all my girlfriends," he said. "Boy, are they happy. I sure like to make all those poor, lonely women happy. What would they do without me?"

I shook my head. I didn't know. Here before me stood a real humanitarian. "Well, Venus," he said earnestly, "you done me so much good, I thought 'what can I do for Venus when she done so much for me? She's here, all alone, poor lady.' I decided the *least* I could do is let you benefit from the results!"

Thank heaven, George moved to Texas shortly thereafter. He left, sincerely believing that he owed me.

I really like selling herbs. The people who buy and use my herbs just keep me in stitches. There is one lady I especially like. Her name is Grace and she works for the post office. She's sixtyish, but looks more like 50. She gives lavish credit to the herbs.

When I first met Grace she talked so much my ears rang. She never stopped. Each animated slap to her fleshy knee would send her gray curls bouncing. I heard about her ex-husband, and how she'd never marry again. I learned she loved auctions and went every Saturday, storing everything she collected in her home. (I'd love to see her place, but she won't let me. She says she has trouble getting in her front door some nights and half the time she can't find her phone when it rings.)

Grace loves animals and uses herbs on them. We call her the "Animal Herb Lady." One of my favorite stories is about her pet bird. Grace found her little finch flat on the bottom of his cage one day, stretched out on his back and kicking feebly. We all know that once a bird takes sick that's usually the end of it.

But Grace wouldn't stand for his dying. She whipped out some of her herbal preparations and gave that tiny bird an enema! Grace said, "He shot bird-doo clean across his cage. After he unloaded, he hopped up on his perch and started singing. That crazy bird," shouted Grace, "was *constipated!* No bird of mine is going to die because he's constipated. I told him if he does that, again, he gets another enema!"

Grace also has an interesting time on her mail route. She told me about one old lady she got to know. One day, Grace met the old lady at her mailbox, crying, "My husband's real sick. The doctors say he's terminal. He's going to die in three months."

Grace sympathized, "What are they doing for him?"

"Nothing," the old lady replied. "They're going to give him an operation and treatment, but, first, they have to make sure all his papers are in order. They want to make sure we can pay for all this stuff. Meanwhile," she complained, "he's making my life miserable. He won't let me keep my old dog." She reached down and scratched a dingy, black pooch that sidled up to her. She sobbed, "He crabs all the time. He says Fuzzer gets on his nerves, and he wants me to put him to sleep."

Grace was touched. She loves animals and couldn't bear thinking Fuzzer would be put away. He didn't look like he'd be any trouble. "I'll tell you what," she suggested, "I'll take Fuzzer. I'll keep him for you while your husband is ill." She figured she could handle three months with a borrowed dog.

The old lady was ecstatic and grateful. So was the old man who ambled out to join them. Grace, being Grace, had to pump him and find out all about his ailment. He was only too willing to share his miseries with her. "Three months," he whispered, "that's all they say I got. They're gonna operate, but I got to wait until they see someone will pay for this." He spit on the ground and stared into space.

Grace couldn't help herself. "Would you take some herbs?" she asked. "Lots of people take them. The ones I'm thinking of have a long reputation for helping conditions like yours."

The old man looked at her. "Well," she continued, her words tripping over themselves, "they sure wouldn't hurt you! You're just waiting now, anyway. *I'd* do it. I'll bring them by, tomorrow."

And she did. She told me that she took the dog and the old guy took the herbs. He took them faithfully, then went in for his operation. One day, shortly after he'd gone to the hospital, Grace found his wife at the mailbox, tears in her eyes. Grace expected the worst. "Guess what," the old lady said, "the old man went to the hospital and they ran a bunch of tests on him. They can't find anything wrong. They said they must have misdiagnosed. He's fine. He's going to live another twenty years!"

Grace got very excited. "Wow! That's wonderful, I'm so happy for you."

The old lady slammed her hands to her hips and pinned Grace with her eyes. "I ain't," she yelled, "now I don't get my dog back!"

(When Linda, my bookkeeper, read this, she said, "What happened? Didn't she get her dog back?" Linda was very concerned. So, I checked with Grace. The happy ending is that the old man was touched that his wife thought enough of him to give her dog away, so he let her take it back.)

SELLING REVIEW

Let me review a few of the important points of selling.
1. Be sincerely enthusiastic about your product. If you don't believe in it, you won't be able to convince anyone else.
2. Have some business cards made and *don't* keep them to yourself.
3. Get a button made, saying ASK ME ABOUT HERBS or WE HAVE HERBS FOR THAT. Wear it everywhere.
4. Talk to people. Be sincerely interested in their problems. Care about them. Put yourself in their place.
5. Never expect people to remember you. Be willing to take the first step in contacting them again. Identify yourself. Be sure you have their name and phone number. Carry pen and paper with you everywhere.
6. *Never* prescribe or diagnose. Leave that to the doctors. Your job is to educate and to provide the herbs your customers ask for. If a person tells you his symptoms, always ask if he's consulted a doctor. If he hasn't, recommend that he do so. Don't take chances with another person's life.
7. Make a card file on each customer. Keep it up to date, call your customers frequently.
8. Last of all, selling takes energy. Constantly work on your own health. Be an example of how health and vitality is gained through the use of herbs.

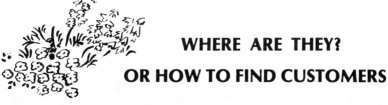

WHERE ARE THEY?
OR HOW TO FIND CUSTOMERS

Now I'm sure you're anxious to know how I find so many interesting customers. I don't spend *all* my time in the grocery store. When looking for customers, I go out a lot. At first, especially, people certainly aren't going to come to you. After you get going, you'll get many referrals, but quite a few of these don't call you. Why should they? They don't know you. You could be nuts.

Think of herb selling as FUN. Put on your herb button, stick your pen and writing pad in your pocket and go bowling, dancing or jogging. Keep your eyes open and take every opportunity to talk herbs. Eat lunch where there are people. Talk to the people in the lunch line. Invite a friend or someone you would like to have as a friend out to lunch. Talk about herbs and the fabulous things that have happened to you while taking them. Overwhelm them with funny herb stories, and bubble with enthusiasm.

Go to the chamber of commerce and ask for a list of all the clubs in town. Find several you would like to join, then do it or at least go look them over. You'll make contacts and have a good time. Write letters to the others. Tell them you're available to talk to their group about herbs and tell them your experiences with herbs. No charge. You can pick up numerous new clients at a lecture. Be sure to call a week or so after the letter goes out. Offer to meet with a club member, so they'll know you're all there. Because they're wondering if you are. They don't know you.

ME? TALK ABOUT HERBS?

Maybe you're thinking, "*I* could never give a talk about herbs. Especially to strangers. And, I don't know anything, yet! This may work for Venus, but she's different."

I'm *not* different. When I first started, I didn't know anything, but it never occurred to me to act like I didn't.

One of the very first distributors I signed up was an author who was quite used to lecturing, traveling and being in front of the public. She asked me if I would speak to a group about herbs, if she got it together. I said, "Sure." I didn't tell her I had never, ever, spoken to a group before. She just assumed I did it all the time. I didn't want to tell her any different.

I supposed she'd get five or six people, I'd pretend they were all my buddies and we'd be fine. I gathered some notes on different peoples' results with herbs (always interesting), carried some herb books with me and figured this would be easy-pie.

When I got to the address she'd given me, I realized it was a meeting hall. I felt a little uneasy, but went on in. There sat 50 people, at least. I started to tremble. Cari had advertised in the *newspaper*; apparently telling how knowledgeable I was about herbs (several cases of diarrhea and one very heavy cleansing cold qualified me). Everyone had come to hear me, be impressed and ask questions. As Cari introduced me, she made me sound like the LAST AND ONLY herb authority. (As she told me later, "It never hurts to expand and expound on your qualifications when you're writing a book jacket blurb, doing a lecture, writing an ad or introducing a speaker."

These people were looking at an Herb Goddess (me). My simple, handwritten testimonials were in tatters, my sweaty hands had eaten right through them. As I approached the podium and stood before the group, I began to feel dizzy. I could feel myself listing to the left. I thought, "How am I going to get through this?" I was panicky. My mind seemed to be just to the right side of my body as I began to talk. I just talked and talked, while the other part of me listened and thought, "Whatever is she saying?" I made it through, and Cari got herb orders, so I guess everything went okay.

That experience taught me what I needed to know. I decided right there that I would never be frightened out of my wits again. If I wanted to specialize in being frightened, I could, but if I did, I'd never make it in the herb business. So, I stopped. I took control. I made a vow that I would speak and speak and lecture and talk until it was easier than sliding downhill. And now it is. I love it.

But to get back to finding prospects. Grocery stores are not the only place to find customers. EVERYONE is a prospect. At one point, I was so busy selling herbs and had so many new people that I felt sure I was acquainted with almost everyone in town. I felt there just couldn't be any more places to look for clients. I was wrong. As my husband and I stood in a long movie line one day, I felt overwhelmed. "All of these people live near me and are potential buyers, and I don't know a soul! There must be thousands more in town, just like them," I thought. My heart began racing with anticipation. I could trot down the whole movie line, talking herbs, and probably sell 75 percent.

For occasions like this, I always try to carry some herb samples that work quickly. (NOT bowel cleansers.)

It's hard to impress people with something that's going to make them feel invincible ... in two years. I carry a little bottle of herbal oil that was formulated by an old Chinese herbalist, long ago in China. Its ingredients are secret; but I've found it almost always gives instant results. Historically, it relieves the symptoms of headaches in about two minutes, the same for nausea, sore throats, car sickness, dizziness, arthritic pains, sinus, etc. Let your future customer rub that on their problems. If they get instant relief, you have an instant convert. They can *feel* that herbs work. I also carry the herbs that traditionally give energy. When a person takes them and, shortly after, feels steam shooting out of their kettle ... they're sold.

Everyone is a prospect. Always keep that idea in mind. Here's an example: Two lovely ladies used to come to my door, every week. They belonged to one of the religions that make housecalls and hope to help you see the Light. I, personally, feel I already see the Way, but I didn't want to hurt their feelings. I knew they believed deeply in their religion and only wanted to help me. But I was getting real tired of standing in my doorway for an hour every week, listening to stories about hell and getting the peewadem scared out of me.

So, one day, I greeted them with a big grin and said, "Hi! Why don't you come in and have some tea?"

They exchanged looks that said, "Thank heaven, we've made an inroad here!" I could see their relief. Two months of standing on my doorstep and, at last, they were going to save me. (But, I bet you folks know me pretty well by now. I had plans to save THEM.)

I led them (the innocents) into my kitchen and settled them at my table. We all got cozy with some herbal tea. We exchanged a few weather-related thoughts and then I laid it out, "I used to be sick all the time," I began. "I used to look rotten, too." As they sat mystified, I launched into a 15-minute recital of all my old symptoms; the doctors I'd seen; the tests I'd had; the fatal pronouncements of death, disaster, hypochrondria; my emergency D&C's; my medications. Listen, I did a thorough job on them.

Then, as they sat wondering why I was still alive, I came in with the Miracle Story. How I'd taken herbs and recovered, completely. Not only recovered, but got good looking, as well. How I had lost inches from my waist and hips; grown bosoms; got thick hair; long, hard nails; pretty skin with rosy color; my marriage had improved and I was happy as a songbird. Praise the Lord! The ladies were stunned.

And did they have problems? You bet. By the time I hustled them out the door, they each had a grocery bag full of herb products. They were two surprised ladies. I'll tell you one thing: they've never come back. They know if they do, they'll leave with two more bags. I either cured them or scared them, I don't know which. That's one follow-up I

25

didn't make.

Another example: Summer had a sore throat one day, so I kept her out of school for a week, while I did some heavy cleaning on her. (We also just enjoyed each other's company.) When I returned her to school, I had to take a note to the office explaining her absence.

Now, a week is a long time for a kid to be sick, and the two women in the office knew Summer had been out that long. Most herb ladies would have crept in and left a little note and hoped no one would notice her child dared get a sniffle. Not me. I took some of my herb flyers and marched right in. "Hi. I've had Summer out of school. I gave her a real good cleanse with herbs. I brought you some flyers you might like." I let the top flyer drift onto the table in front of them. That flyer covered all the combinations we had, and what they historically did.

While the two ladies obligingly looked, I began to rattle off my successes with herbs and those of other people I know. Pretty soon, the blonde lady lifted her head, "I want the one for sex," she said.

"Wonderful. No problem," I said. I started slapping my thighs, "I used to have cellulite, but when I went on an herb program, it all melted away!"

"The blonde lady lifted her head, again, "I want that herb," she added. I just talked and smiled and shook my heavy head of hair and clicked my hard nails on the counter.

As I left, the blonde lady was running off copies of the flyers for her friends. The other lady had requested the herbs historically used for fat and promised to tell her sister about me. When the ladies start using the herbs (and I'll keep in touch with them, remember) and see results, you can bet I'll get lots of referrals. All because of one sore throat, that, actually, kind of embarrassed me. But, I make it a habit to always go *around* obstacles or seemingly difficult situations. It's a challenge.

What if the office ladies had ignored my pitch? I would have just laughed. After all, I'd given it my best shot. Laugh at yourself and situations. Don't be afraid to look strange.

When I was a teenager, I was crying one day because I didn't like the way I looked. My hair was wrong, my dress was wrong, everything about me was "ugly." I whined and complained until my mother swung around with total frustration, "Will you stop that! Nobody's even going to notice you, anyway!" I was stunned. I shut up, too.

Years later, I realized what she was saying. "Everyone is so super concerned about THEMSELVES and how *they* look, that you could lace bats in your hair and shove whistles up your tu-tu and no one would notice." So, don't be shy about looking stupid.

SPEAKING OF FLYERS

When I'm out shopping for customers or when they come to me, I always give them a flyer or two. Flyers are simply a piece of paper with typed information about an herb or herbal combination. You can write them yourself or collect information out of herb magazines (just make sure you give credit to your source). When writing them yourself, make sure you use "traditionally" and "historically" in all the right spots and don't diagnose or prescribe. Just present knowledge. Educate. It's a good idea to put a notice at the bottom, something like: "We make no claims, therapeutic or otherwise, for our herbs, we merely report their historical uses." Cite authorities, if you have them. You might also throw in that they should see a doctor if they have a problem. Adjust the wording to what seems right. You have to do this to protect yourself and possibly protect your buyer.

Herb flyers will help your business. One lady was coming to see me for almost two years. She was using herbs faithfully, but couldn't get her husband to try them. We discussed that man up and down, but couldn't crack him. He was afraid he'd be poisoned. He'd drive her over to my house and sit in the car and wait for her. I never saw or met him. His wife told me he was deathly afraid of me. He'd never seen or spoken to me, but he knew for a fact that I was a witch. He meant it, too.

One day, Ellen happened to take several flyers home with her. One was on licorice, the other on gotu kola. The next time I saw her, she had a big grin. "Guess what?" she beamed. "John read those flyers and he wants me to get him some licorice and gotu kola." We both leaped and clapped hands. Another disbeliever had joined us.

27

 # MONEY

"Okay," you say, "if I can get over being shy about selling someone herbs, I still feel *guilty*. Here they are, these poor sick people, and I'm selling them something I should be giving them. Or, at least, giving them at my cost. It's immoral to take money from needy people. How can you do it?"

I used to feel that way. I sure don't any more. First of all, I don't feel like a hustler. I truly believe I'm doing Mother Nature's work. I've told people about herbs, something they may have known nothing about. I've exposed them to something which has been here and used for thousands of years. Only recently — the last 100 years or less — have they been pushed aside. I may even have changed a person's entire life by teaching them simple ways they can help themselves.

Look at it this way. Your body is like your car. It's a vehicle for you to get around in. You take good care of your car and regularly have it checked, oiled, lubed, etc. If you don't, you know that shiny little creature is going to fall apart and make you mad. Why don't you treat yourself at least as well as you treat your car? Why do you wait until your crankshaft is falling out, then run and have it temporarily glued up? Why not try herbs? Herbs are food. They give the body the resources it needs to *repair* itself. They don't cover up the damage. If the herbs go in before the engine blows, maybe it won't blow, huh? It's called preventative maintenance.

Feel guilty about selling herbs? No way!

I used to feel bad about selling retail, though. I'd think, "This person really needs the herbs. They say they don't have the money. I should be good and kind and give them the herbs at my cost. I shouldn't make money from the herbs. They're a sacred thing."

So, I sold wholesale for quite a while. Until I noticed that these people, who couldn't afford to pay me, could afford to go to movies. They could buy big televisions, candy bars and hair ribbons. I also noticed that it was costing me gas money to deliver the herbs. I was spending a lot of money buying herb books to study, going to classes, spending hours and days researching, using the telephone, giving out flyers and using up my life to help people.

I figured all that was worth something. I realized I *deserved* to sell retail. If I didn't, I was going to lose money, go out of business and then be UNABLE TO HELP ANYONE. That settled it for me. I hope it does for you, too. I also found I needed retail money to build my stock. If you have the herb products on hand, you will sell much more. People are hot to buy when they're hot. Not next week.

MORE ABOUT
MONEY

It's a touchy subject — money. I don't believe money is the root of all evil, but it can sure cause a flap. True to form, I have had many problems with money.

When you become a distributor, the first thing you have to do is set up a separate bank account for your herbs. If you get your money all mixed up, you won't know if you're gaining or losing. Go to your local bank and tell them you want a business account. I got one of those large checkbooks with three checks to a page and a side for writing what's been spent and where. It's large enough that it's a bit harder for me to misplace.

Everything having to do with the herb business must go through this account. You'll then have a record of all your transactions. If you see too much is going out, you can catch it before it's too late. You have to know where all your money is going. Keep a journal or a daily notebook, so you know what you're spending and where.

Keep track of all your write-offs for taxes. You will need a little book to carry everywhere, to record all monies spent for gas, distributor lunches, advertising, postage, door prizes, education, etc. Send for the free booklet from the U.S. government, *Tax Guide for Small Businesses*. At the end of every month, write yourself a check on your business account for all the out-of-pocket expenses so you will have a record.

When I first started, I realized I couldn't pull much, if any, money out of the business. I needed every cent to build up my stock and acquire the equipment needed for my office. This is one reason why retail sales can be important. It's gravy money to grow on.

When I first started in the herb business, I decided I would work incredibly hard for two years and expect nothing. I would work morning, noon and night. The third year, I would sit back a bit and start gathering in some profits. That's just what I've done, and it has worked well. You have to be able to visualize the future and not be discouraged by the present.

It's a good idea to have a regular part-time job or working spouse while you're building the business. Peace of mind is a friendly co-worker.

When I first started my business, I made some big mistakes. Very big. You may, too. Don't give in, like so many other people. Just recognize what you've done, give it a kick and walk around it. One lesson I learned was: don't give credit. I've lost thousands of dollars that way, mostly to my "friends."

There was one fellow, Bill, who signed with me. He was crazy about herbs and the business. He was leaving for Louisiana to visit all his relatives and begged for a load of products. He assured me he'd mail the money from Louisiana when he sold it to all the home folks who were waiting with lolling tongues for the herbs. He meant it, too. He was very sincere. He took $300 worth of herbs with him. I've never seen him since. I heard he got jailed in Georgia for drunk driving, and all his belongings were stolen. I heard that, but I've never heard a word from Bill.

Another lady was such a sweetheart. She was having a rough time. She was so poor, she kept getting her electricity turned off and she had lots of physical problems. I often took her food packages. She didn't have a job because she couldn't seem to find one that quite suited her, and she wasn't quite ready to work, yet, anyway. But, she was such a sweet lady and she did need help so badly, and she was so grateful when I'd give her herbs on credit. She put her house up for sale and assured me that as soon as it sold she'd pay me right off. We were the best of friends.

Well, she sold that house and was gone in two days. I got a sweet note from her telling me how much she appreciated me; but she'd had to pay her lawyer and everyone else from the escrow check and there was nothing left for me. She assured me that she surely would pay and not to doubt her; she surely would. Her address was general delivery and the letter I wrote her came back. I've never heard from her since. It's been almost two years and I'm out $400+. You want to hear more? I can tell you more, because I don't learn easy.

Another very nice woman, alone and struggling to raise two children, wanted to become a manager. I said she couldn't become a manager until she paid me off. (You see, I was getting tougher.) She owed me about $1,000. She was really anxious to become a manager, so she borrowed the money. Somehow she talked me into letting her pay the bill down to $300 and giving her the "go-sign" for manager. I did. It's been two years now, and I've never seen the money.

I get a lot of promises. "I'll pay you $10 a week" or "$20 a month." Then, "I need to take the kids on holiday and we won't be back for four months, so I can't pay anything for a while. Deals like that, but no money. Finally, I got disgusted and laid it all out in a letter. I got a very shocked letter in return. Of course, she planned to pay — things had been tough — so sorry that I was upset, our friendship was very important, etc. I didn't reply. I did get a very nice Christmas card, but I've never seen a cent.

In any business, I suppose, you learn a person's true character. It hurts to know it, sometimes.

When you take an order, get the money *then*. With new customers you might want to say, "My herb lady has to have the money." If mailing, mail COD, or get the money, first. It's real hard for people to pay for something that's already used and gone.

Accurate accounting is a must. When you or your distributor write an order, make sure you check it carefully. I had to retire an adding machine that made $1,000 mistakes. I've often forgotten to add tax or shipping.

When your people pay for an order, staple their check to your copy or write their check number on it if they pay by check; write cash, if they pay in cash. That way you'll know you remembered to collect the money. I accept postdated checks. A check in hand is much better than one that will be sent later. Some managers and distributors put a license number on the check, or the name of the person who sent them over if they don't know the customer.

Remember, people who ask you to give credit often let the bill slide for months and months and months. You're not their banker. You're not in business to loan the money. You don't even require interest. They're *using* you. Notice how often they pay everyone else off, or trip down to Mexico and leave your bill unpaid.

You need to teach your distributors about money. I have distributors who are dynamic, super sales people. They do immense volume, yet they never have any money and are deeply in debt. I've had them sit and cry in my office, complaining they're not making any money. They say, "I work and work and never get anywhere." It's a simple matter of not knowing how to manage their money. They know how to sell, but they don't know what they're doing businesswise.

For example, when I first started doing business, I gave credit freely, as I've said. One outstanding lesson I learned was from Mary. Whenever Mary came to pick up herbs and couldn't pay for them, I'd say, "Thats okay, you can pay me when you get the money." Sometimes I'd get checks from her, mostly I wouldn't. Sometimes she would pay a little cash. All very innocent. Mary was a super salesperson. She had a good heart and really meant to pay me. I didn't worry. One day I added up the bill. It was $1,700. I screamed and so did Mary. She took to her bed after begging me never to tell her husband.

I didn't hear from Mary for several weeks. She'd totally given up on herb selling and confined herself to her home. I told her, "Mary,

31

we've got to work this out. I don't want you to quit selling herbs. You're fantastic at selling herbs. You have a real talent and you're going to pay me off!'' After many tears, Mary went back to selling herbs. She's now paid me completely and is one of my super star managers. There's a moral here: Cash on the line.

SAVINGS

I plan for my future. I have no intention of being a little old lady, living with dirty carpets and eating dogfood and bird seed. I always set aside some money out of everything I make. When my bonus check comes in, I skim, right off the top, whatever I feel comfortable with. I bank it and never even consider it when I'm down to the wire in my business or personal bills. That money is my future. I make a game of saving money. It's a big thrill to see how much I can squeeze out of the business. When I have enough saved, I invest in real estate, stock, T.D.'s, silver, gold, a new rug, a trip to Bakersfield or whatever seems good to me and my family. Life changes. I might not be selling herbs in two years. Then, my income might be coming in from my investments.

Saving money gives me a feeling of freedom. My husband has been very good about my penchant for security. I have an acre of land in my name only and some stock. You never know what may happen. It's good for a woman to have something of her own. It's much harder for a woman than a man to make a living if there's a divorce, a separation or a death, because she often has children and, perhaps, few marketable skills. Also, sadly, women don't get equal pay with men, even though they may have to support a family and pay for child care, too.

Some people have a real fear of success. When the herb money starts rolling in, they panic and draw back. They're doing "too well." Success scares them. Why? Maybe they're used to being unsuccessful. Having money and power is a heady feeling. It's new. You have to ease into and get used to having money. Don't pull back just because it's an unknown. Analyze your fears. Accept your new place in life, pat yourself on the back and enjoy. It's okay to be successful and have money.

Other people feel extremely guilty about actually making a living by helping people. It seems somehow unChristian. Would God have us suffer while helping the suffering? Accept the fruit of your labors!

MANAGERSHIP

I was a distributor only three weeks before I realized I should be a manager. Managers no longer get products from their sponsors, they order direct from the company and make bigger bonuses. They also deal with and keep track of more people, more money and more paperwork. They are responsible for collecting and paying state taxes. In order to do this, they must obtain a resale license (in California). The laws are different in other states. Contact the local state Board of Equalization office for information.

That is easy enough, but I'm going to tell you how to do it the hard way. The way my brother, Arthur, and I did it.

When both he and I started our separate businesses, our family said, "You two had better get your tax numbers. You've got to pay state taxes on what you sell!" What? This was news to us. We got more advice. We were told horrifying stories by people who had applied for the tax number and had paid hundreds of dollars for the license. Art and I sure didn't want to pull all that money out of our nearly empty pockets just for the privilege of paying even more later.

We were told, "Act stupid. For gosh sakes don't act like you're making a lot of money. Don't act like you know what you're doing. Be docile. Be agreeable. If you work it right, you won't have to put any money down. You'll be able to get the license FREE, so you can pay the state money." Such a deal.

Art and I weren't too excited about making the hour-long trip to San Diego. We didn't relish, first of all, *finding* the building, then driving around and around it hoping for a parking space, then locating the correct room and looking and acting like two semi-nerds. But, we did it. After making our appearances in several government offices, we finally found the right one. We gave each other a nudge in the ribs and ambled in. After trying to fill out an unfillable form, we were called, separately, into various offices.

I sat across a desk from a pregnant girl with kitchen-broom hair. She was determined to be all business. With studied country charm I slipped my sandals off, hiked up my jeans a bit and gave her a big smile. She pointed out the blanks I had left unanswered on the form. I continued smiling and ineptly filled in the spaces. As she shuffled papers and snapped business questions at me, I continued to look friendly and, I hoped, like the average Ms. Housewife.

What kind of business did I do? "Oh, I sell herbs ... I sell herbs from my house." I shrugged my shoulder and looked apologetic, as if to say, "Yeah, I know. I'll never make a dime selling herbs. I just need something to do." The girl looked at me. I continued my mental conversation. "Yes, I know. It's really dumb...." I let my eyes fall to my feet. Then I lifted them to ask a few simple-minded questions. I tell you, I was a star. I polished off my performance by asking about her pregnancy, then reminiscing about mine.

By then, I felt so confident, I asked HER a question I knew SHE couldn't answer. This sent her scurrying out into other offices, asking her superiors. None of them knew the answer, either, which caused a muffled row behind the partitions. I smiled smugly. This had been fun. The girl came back and gave me the license — no charge. She handed me a form I was to fill out every three months. That form *did* genuinely confuse me. She then told me I was to send all my collected state taxes in at intervals. I was free to go. Simple.

I trotted out of her office and went to find Art. I found him out in the hall, storming up and down, blustering and blathering. He has tremendous vocal volume. I couldn't make out what his problem was, but I thought I'd better get him out of there. I grabbed his elbow as we flailed toward the elevators. Art's arms were spinning like wheels, his brows were laced together and he was sputtering incoherently. As we stepped into the elevator, an enraged bellow exploded from him, "THAT GIRL! SHE WOULDN'T GIVE IT TO ME! She said I had no business applying for a license. She said I didn't even know what I was DOING!"

I was open-mouthed. "You mean, Art," I asked, "you acted TOO dumb?" I couldn't believe it. Everyone has to have that license to pay state taxes. Arthur had been refused. That woman refused to allow Art to pay taxes. All the way home Art hollered at me and pounded the dash, while I laughed.

Yes, Art finally got his license. He waited a few weeks, calmed down and then went to a different office where he appeared perfectly normal.

OFFICE ORGANIZATION
— MY HERB ROOM

When I first started my herb business I made do. I chose a little-used room upstairs and stored my herbs in a tiny, one-door closet with three 2'x3' shelves. It was dark in that closet and a real chore to put the herbs in and take them out. To make it easier, I took a felt pen and wrote the name of the herb on top of the bottle.

When I became a manager and the business grew larger, I got fancier. I chose a few boxes that were sectioned off and stood them on each shelf, facing me, to give me more room. I stored herbs in the sections and herbs on top of the boxes.

The closet was just big enough to put my head and torso in, and invariably as I leaned into the shelves, the door would whack me on the back. After diving head first into my herbs 50 times, I decided I needed REAL shelves. I may have many talents, but carpentry is not one of them. However, I rarely consider that I cannot do something, so I go ahead and do it.

I bought five long, heavy shelf boards at the local store and three long wall bars and 12 "thingers" to hold the shelves up. Also some screws. Getting all this stuff into my car was difficult enough, how I ever thought I could actually put up shelves is beyond me.

I got home and lugged those suckers upstairs. I chose a wall and planned my design. I used a ruler and a pencil. I knew enough to guess I'd better if I wanted the shelves to sit straight. First, I put the wall bars up. I found the screws wouldn't screw in, so I took a nail and hammered some holes for the screws. Then I remembered reading that you have to hang shelves from the wall studs. I also knew those studs were in the wall, somewhere. I've seen men tap, tap, tap the walls, look very wise, stop and pound a nail. That's what I did. Tap, tap, tap, tap. It all sounded the same to me. I spent about half an hour tapping and listening and finally decided it was just an old wive's tale that carpenters passed around in order to stay busy.

I pounded my nails and screws where they looked best and slipped those shelf thingers into the slots and lifted on the boards. It looked good to me. Oh, sure, some boards were a little crooked, but so what?

I had five wonderful shelves that I'd made myself. I was very proud. I used those shelves for about a year and a half. They held all the products I put on them, and I often mentioned to people — especially Keith — how clever I had been to find the studs. Keith was very impressed.

One day I went upstairs to fiddle in the herb room. It was Sunday and Keith was watching football in the living room. I'll do almost anything to get away from a TV set that plays football all day, so I'd decided to work. Anyway, I had a shipment of herbs to unpack and shelve. So, that's what I did. I spent about an hour unpacking and stacking the lot, putting them beside the rest of my stock.

I had just put my last bottle of aloe vera juice on the shelf, then paused to admire my collection, when, by heaven, I simply couldn't believe it, those shelves sprang forward from the wall and attacked me. I was literally too stunned and shocked to move.

With an absolutely tremendous roar, about $20,000 worth of products and boards hit me. I was knocked to the floor and buried in spinning, clacking herb bottles. Quarts of bentonite struck and bounced off me; one crashed into a writing pen and began shooting a steady arc of liquid clay across the room. Bottles slammed together and rained capsules and powdered herbs on me and the walls. It all happened and ended in seconds.

I lay on my back, stunned and covered with herb dust, bottles and cans. Keith just about broke his neck running upstairs. He thought a jet had hit the house and killed me. He kept asking if I was all right. I couldn't even speak. He helped me to bed, where I lay for an hour.

To make everything worse, just before my shelves collapsed, Keith had been building me another set in a large closet at the other side of the room. He's not known for his manual skills either and had been piddling along for two months. Summer and I had been giving him a lot of static. He'd go into the herb room to work, and Summer and I would try to disappear. First, he removed the closet doors, which was trauma enough. Then he spent several weeks cutting and exactly matching some green and yellow foil self-stick wallpaper to the back and side walls of the closet.

There was much cursing and yelling and demanding from him. "Where's my tape? Who took the ruler? There's not enough of this paper! Who took some?" He'd have me stand for hours, holding a piece of foil which he slowly — very slowly — matched and trimmed then thought about the effect of that piece there. I'd finally say I had things to do and he'd reply, "Well, if you can't help me — if you don't care — then forget it."

After two weeks he finally got the wallpaper exactly matched and hung and we all came in and admired his work and praised him mightily. He did do a marvelous job. Unfortunately, when we got up in the morning and dutifully trooped in to admire it, again, most of it had fallen off the wall. I don't need to tell you about how bad the shelf project became after that.

He, too, had to find the studs in the wall. He spent days and nights tapping and yelling. It didn't help any that *my* shelves still hung serenely — at that time — at the other end of the room, crowded with herbs. He kept tapping and complaining, "I can't believe *you* found those studs! You had someone help you. You *couldn't* have found them." Tap, tap, tap. "I can't find the @#%&*! things!" Summer said later that he kept her awake nights. She could hear him through the bedroom wall, tapping and pounding, muttering, swearing and throwing things.

I'm sure it was a great relief to him when my shelves finally collapsed. Apparently he eventually found the studs, because his shelves are still up and we've had many compliments on them. Sure, there are a few paint spills on the rug where he fell off a stool and flipped a can of paint, but, so what?

After the shelves were settled, I also commandeered an old desk and an equally old adding machine (check your newspaper for garage and estate sales). I put a few pictures on the walls and I was in business.

Once you get a room to yourself, you might consider these ideas:

Get a pretty teapot and start collecting unusual cups. You can serve hot herb teas to your people. (Of course, this is a poor idea if you find they hang around all day and drink, and you can't get your work done.) I also like the idea of a woodburning stove or even a fake fireplace. People will want to come to your place. It and you will be so comfortable and cheery. I also like to put green and flowering plants throughout the room; it makes it feel like "Herb Land."

I have a new herb room, now, where the garage used to be. This room has shelves of herbs and related books, which are used often as references or for pure enjoyment and education.

I like to sell books at cost or close to it because once people educate themselves they'll buy your products because they know how to use them. I also have a shelf of books which I call my lending library. On this shelf I also have herbal education tapes by such people as LaDean Griffin, Dr. J.R. Christopher and myself. (I tape some of the Herb and Sales and Motivation classes.)

I have stacks of herb magazines and many flyers on various herbs and combinations of herbs. I used to line my piles of flyers on the floor, but that got out of hand. Now, I use small cardboard boxes that can be stacked one on top of the other and are easily accessible.

Try and have some comfortable furniture. It doesn't have to be gorgeous. I have an old kelly-green chair. Kids love to pull the foam out of its stuffed and tattered arms. This chair came from my first marriage. The salesman assured us it was a "real pecan wood chair that will grow old with you." The "pecan" started wearing off the basic plastic in three weeks, and the marriage in due course wore off, too. But, you get the idea about the furniture the herb room has. You could find better in a swap meet, but nobody seems to mind!

And, of course, we have shelves — good *solid* shelves — loaded with herbs. I have small sticky tags with my name, address and phone number. When I pluck herbs off the shelves for retail people, I put these tags on the bottles. When the bottle is empty, they will know who to call.

Of course, we keep bags for all the herbs that are trundled off. I use regular lunch bags and old grocery bags.

I have a small desk that I use for wrapping UPS packages and a large one that's always loaded with my "important" stuff.

I finally bought a file cabinet so I can keep a FEW things straight, and I suggest you do the same. Right away. Don't wait, like I did, until you're going nuts with piles of papers. I still like to store things I just *might* need, soon, at my feet under my desk, although I think this annoys Linda, my bookkeeper. She tries to keep everything picked up and filed, and I insist on this heavy, dusty rat's nest under my desk. I also specialize in kicking it when I'm working, and this gets it all tangled up together.

In my file cabinet I keep legal-size folders all labeled subject wise: flyers to rework, herb articles, accounts receivable, herb orders, back orders, etc. Anything that can be filed, we try and file. I also keep large manila envelopes in this cabinet. They are marked by month and year, helping me keep the business together at month's end.

I keep a small file box on top of my desk with all distributors' and retailers' addresses. I also keep a junk box full of junk papers that may be valuable. I've had a rubber stamp made with my name and address which I use to stamp anything that needs stamping. I even stamp kids if they'll hold their hand out. This way I get walking advertising.

After months and months of driving 40 miles to my folks to use their typewriter to type the newsletter, I shopped around and got a refurbished electric one that seems just as good as a new one and cost less.

There's also a large bulletin board on the wall and a chalkboard. The bulletin board displays things like articles on selling, herb newsletters from group members, the company magazine, cards demanding that you persist and never give up, class schedules, etc. I use the chalkboard for classes and whatever needs illustrating — like bowels.

When you start selling herbs and building a group, you will suddenly notice how many kids there are in the world and in your house. Not only have our aquarium fish been bagged, but our color TV has had its tuning knobs adjusted and removed by five year olds; and Summer lost her collector's sugar Easter egg with inner pictures. Someone ate it. I've found kids standing on our couch, peeling nailed pictures off the walls, or squashing oranges and bananas into the rug. This just happens. You and the mother get excited about the herbs, and the kids just drift off to find something *they* find interesting. I now provide their excitement — special toys in the herb room, a playpen — and a sign on the door to the rest of the house that says, "OFF LIMITS." (Sign, courtesy of Summer.)

It's a nice idea to have a basket full of people's bottled worms and gallstones in your herb room. This seems to impress people. They suddenly seem real anxious to get on an herb program.

Some herb sellers keep photo books full of newspaper and magazine clippings, relating to the herbs, pertinent health topics and damage by drugs and surgery. Clients can browse through these when they are through looking at bottled liver flukes and tapeworms. When new people come to buy herbs, you can also show them slides on herbs, vitamins, iridology or any products your company carries.

Many times I hand out herb samples and sometimes loan one of the mini-tramps. I also loan the person a book on the small trampoline and tell them to read the testimonials, first. (This gets them so excited they have to read the dull parts.) Then, as I wave them off, rebounder under their arms, I say, "You can keep the trampoline and book for three days! I'll call you and see what you think." I do. Most of them buy the tramp. Don't wait more than three or four days, though. Enthusiasm wanes and you may lose the sale.

Instead of popcorn, pass out product samples. Your customers will have a wonderful time. For the price of a few herbs, they'll have had a better time than going to the movies or to a carnival together. And, they'll send their friends to you.

EDUCATION (TRAINING)

Now you know about money and your herb room or working area. What do you know about what you're selling?

When I first started herb work, as you know, I didn't know anything about herbs; but I didn't let that stop me. People say, "I can't sell herbs. I don't know anything about herbs."

I say, "Neither does anyone else."

Get books on herbs (see bibliography). Read everything you can about them. Learn everything you can about your company. Read books on salesmanship and apply it to your product. Get training in any field that will touch on your product: iridology, kinesiology, Touch for Health, herbology. Take classes from herbalists, doctors, lay people or local colleges — anyone who can help you with your work. The books, classes and travel are a tax write-off. Enjoy yourself; keep your mind open. Learn as much as you can about everything, but don't get pulled off your main line of work or you'll be just like everyone else. And you want to be at the *top!*

The diplomas you collect will look good on your wall. Some people are even impressed by them. You must educate yourself by whatever honest means you can, and if it takes diplomas, get them.

When I have to, I'll drop "Big Names" I've worked with, been taught by or know. I'll even sidle up to a diploma on my wall and lean against it, maybe even drape an arm around it. Point right to it and tap it, if it's necessary. Like I said, some people will only give you credibility if "Higher Lights" have seemingly shone on you.

To make the herb business work, you *must* educate people. This is the key to your success. Educate yourself as you go along. Don't wait to start until you're educated or you'll never start.

I go to all our company conventions. I go for business reasons. I spend my time talking to other distributors and managers and asking questions about how they run their groups. I play fair, though, and tell them how I run mine. I always try to talk to the people who have a brilliant track record. I force myself because sometimes I feel timid around these splendid folk. However, when I sit down and look, un-emotional and unawed, at many of these top people, I'm impressed by how average some of them seem. There appear to be few genuises among them. They make me feel right at ease. I think this may be part of their studied charm and success. The average person looks at them, feels right at home, even superior and says, "I can do what *they do,* for gawds' sake!"

At these conventions, I don't spend all my time with the "stars."

Everyone there has ideas. The skinny lady from Teetotum, Arkansas, may have a headful of ingenious thoughts.

Never pass up opportunities to learn from other multi-level organizations. I attend almost anything that gets too close to me. I not only learn their successful secrets, but after people in those groups have solicited me, I solicit *them*. I have a number of people in my organization who swore they'd never sell herbs.

Along with teaching Basic Classes (Chapters 18-19), I also teach an Herb Education Class, the first and third Thursdays at the local library. This runs from 7:30 to 9 p.m. I encourage my distributors to come and bring people. I don't sell herbs at the class. I just teach historical facts about different herbs, combinations and problems.

Sometimes I'll show a filmstrip about the company and extol our herbs' superior virtues. (The library will now know why their clock is occasionally haywire in the morning. I usually get the plugs confused when hooking up the projector.) At other times I will show slides on herbs or iridology.

I work to keep my classes entertaining. By 7:30 it's often dark and cold. In homes everywhere, TV pictures are leaping and cavorting, husbands are sleeping on the couches and kids are busy smearing peanut butter under the chair seats. It's difficult and uncomfortable for people to get out of the house. Especially to sit on a hard chair for an hour and a half and LEARN something. I know this, and I sincerely appreciate everyone who gets themselves to my classes. I tell them so. I also tell many anecdotes and testimonials. I read some herb information, but break it up with free-form talk. I write on the blackboard, stand up, sit down, hold in my stomach, yell at my daughter if she's being obstreperous and, generally, keep the people awake. I take every opportunity to be funny and enjoy myself. It seems to work. People tell me quite frequently that it's better than going to a movie.

Sometimes I have distributors or other people speak on herbs. (Generally not more than 15 minutes the first time because you and the audience may start wishing you could pull them off the stage with a hook.) Often, the group will get excited and give their own testimonials. Sometimes they all get so verbal I have to threaten them with a ruler. Other times they just sit there like big silent buzzards. Better that, though, than to have no one show.

So far, I've always had *someone* turn up, but it's been pretty close many times. I just go ahead and teach as if I had 50. Whenever I feel rejected or disappointed by my turnout, I remind myself and my group about another manager, who told us he hired a large hall in a fancy hotel, had it catered and sent out 1,100 special invitations for a super-duper herb meeting. The night of the Grande Affair, two people showed up. My little fizzled affairs have never bothered me after hearing his sad story.

Most of the time I have a minor idea of what I'm going to say at my classes. I used to write everything out word by word by word, and it was dull, dull, dull. Now, I have a simple outline and just let the talk flow from that. I'm as surprised as anyone by the things that come tumbling and sliding out of me.

Sometimes I try to hold a proper meeting. I will be very composed, mature and attempt to overwhelm my class with my knowledge. I especially work to impress when there are new and skeptical folks in the group.

I was doing a good job one night, standing before the class giving an outstanding lecture on the virtues and chemical composition of certain herbs, when my daughter, Summer, crept up to me. I tried to subtly wave her away, but she wouldn't be moved. She grabbed my hair and pulled my head down to hers. She flipped a few shifty looks at the rapt class and whispered, "Mother! Your pants are too short for your boots." She tugged circumspectly at the rear of my pants.

"Summer!" I mouthed, "Get away from me!"

She grabbed my ear and whispered urgently, "Mother, you look funny." She continued pulling my pants downward.

"For heaven's sake Summer," I exploded, "get, get." I turned a fake smile to the amused audience. I had to tell them. "My pants are too short for my boots," I said. The class craned their neck to look. "I look funny," I sighed and we continued with one of my irregular, regular classes.

When the business slows down or I get bored or my people do, I usually change my classes. At the moment, along with the Basic Classes and the two Herb Education Classes, I run a meeting in my herb room every Monday morning before I open for business. The class starts at 9. This is a Sales and Motivation Class and draws the hard core, senior members of my group. We spend an hour discussing our successes from the past week, giving each other suggestions, learning different multi-level and sales techniques and renewing our excitement about herbs. We drink herb tea and just lay back and have a nice time. It's a good place to bring potential or new serious distributors. We infect them with our drive and ambition. Sometimes we have a rousing "rah-rah" class — whatever fits.

Once a month we have a potluck for distributors and managers. These are always well attended. People come because they want to eat. The potlucks are held on a Monday night from 7 to 9.

I usually have an on-time drawing. The prize is a nice product gift, and I advertise it as I give it away. Then we eat. About 8, I teach company business, iridology, product knowledge or whatever needs to be discussed. If you can't hold your classes in your home, look to churches or go to your local chamber of commerce. They have a list of all available meeting spaces, including banks, restaurants and others.

I always have a list of my classes with dates printed in my newsletters. But, not everyone reads my newsletter. (I'm always threatening to quiz them about contents and sometimes I do. I also hide contests or information they need to know inside. I do whatever I have to, to keep my group moving!)

People need to be reminded about my classes. I'll often call several days beforehand to prod them. I use guilt: "Can I *count* on you to be there?" My voice pleads and trembles. "Can I really count on you?"

The cold night of the class comes and they remember, "Oh, gosh, I have to go. Venus is *counting* on me!"

If you would like to teach a class every night of the week and see your business surge ahead, do this: When you sell a friend herbs, ask if they will set up a class for you.

Once you're at the class, mention to each person that you're available to do a class for their friends, too. Give your card. Take their names and numbers, then call them.

If you aren't an iridologist, don't sit down, cry and say, "Oh, I'll never sell herbs. I can't analyze eyes at a class like lots of people do." When I first started, I spoke and sold strictly herbs and did extremely well. The promise of good food, fun and an unusual speaker will bring people.

But, please, don't give people the idea you're coming to sell something. You're coming to teach. It's not your fault if they practically tear your clothes off and beg you for herbs after class.

Another thing. I continually learn all I can about my company and my product. If this means taking a trip to see the company's plant, do it. Or at least read their literature and see their slide/tapes. Learn all you can about their herbs, combinations and related products. For legal reasons, the company can't often tell you much about the herbal combinations or uses of herbs. Use your head and your common sense. Read about each herb and puzzle out how it would work with other herbs. You can often find the answers in newsletters and books.

I have emphasized that I attempt to keep all my classes loaded with information, yet be fun. Sickness is usually seen as a serious and sad business. My philosophy is: if you have to be sick, you might as well enjoy yourself.

Remember, *going to classes and giving classes are a part of the job!*

One subject you might like to study and teach at your classes is iridology ...

IRIDOLOGY

The approach I take to iridology may sound very flip, but here's why it works for me. The average person who comes to me has usually had no contact with iridology, has no knowledge of it, thinks it's odd-ball, or is outright skeptical. Sometimes they're even frightened by the concept. I've had people turn white and say it's the works of the devil, and others back away from me, sure that I'm going to look in their eyes and tell them they have an incurable disease or the details of their sex life.

In the beginning, iridology and I approach people in a light-hearted manner. This puts them at ease and disarms them. They spend a lot of time laughing and end up being amazed by iridology's accuracy. The science of iridology becomes a serious fact to them. Personally, I know iridology is true and real. I hate to read my own eyes. They tell the truth and sometimes that's hard to handle. Iridology has been an invaluable tool in helping me to understand the needs of the people I sell herbs to and, therefore, has helped me build my business. Consider using my approach or use your own. Iridology works, either way.

I used to do many eye readings for people before my hypochondria caught up with me. In one day I could have rabies, cancer, flat feet and be pregnant. Whatever my clients had, I had. It was too hard on me.

One time I got a call from a man. A stranger. He scheduled an appointment to get his eyes analyzed. Now, there was nothing unusual about seeing a man — even a strange one. But I felt uneasy. Very uneasy. As the week wore on, I became more nervous. I was seeing lots of people daily, and I wasn't concerned about *them* or *their* motives. But, I was just sure *this* man was out to get me for some legal offense.

I determined to be more careful than usual. Absolutely no prescribing or diagnosing or even suggesting. I wouldn't even let him *see* my herb room. (Normally I taught in another room so I wouldn't be accused of undue influence with all the herbs lined up behind me.) I wouldn't sell the man herbs if he pleaded and begged. (At this time, it's suggested that you don't sell herbs at the same time you analyze eyes.) I definitely wouldn't write anything down. I'd be sure to ask him, "Are you with the FDA, the California Consumer Affairs Board or any like agency? Are you tape recording me?" I would have him sign a sheet saying I didn't diagnose or prescribe and this was only nutritional counseling. I would be absolutely perfect.

The day came and I was ready. The doorbell rang and I perspired. There stood a neatly suited and tied man, with dark, slicked-back hair. "An accountant. Mr. Johns."

"Ha!," I thought, "sure!"

I led him into my kitchen, sat him down and grilled him. Then I gave him the briefest, barest analysis I ever gave anyone. He watched me, intently. I got an "um" and an "ahmm" out of him, but the rest was just a pair of eyes staring at me.

I was so nervous, if a door had slammed, I would have leaped into the oven. At last, I jumped up from the chair and said loudly, "That's it! So glad you came. Goodbye."

Mr. Johns stood, too, pulling absently at his tie. "Venus," he cleared his throat, "you look so healthy; you have such a pretty body." I was taken aback. He put out his hands and circled them around my middle. "Such a tiny waist," he said. I took several steps back, trailing him with me, prying and gently pushing away his hands. They clung to mine, as he stared at me, dewy-eyed and mesmerized. "You're so pretty. You have such lovely eyes."

A door clicked open and harsh, acid-rock music spilled from my stepson's room. I heard the boy's feet padding toward the kitchen and so did Mr. Johns. I slid him out the front door in two seconds flat. "So nice to have met you," I said.

Then I collapsed with laughter. I had been so nervous. I was sure he was a government agent. Someone out to catch me and turn me in. That's all I could relate to my uneasiness. Instead, he was a lecher — a regular, run-of-the-mill lecher. I almost got raped, not jailed. I was so relieved. This is the only so-called problem I've ever had with people coming to my home, and I consider it only an amusing incident.

Here's something I do that sells a lot of herbs, inspires my distributors and introduces iridology. I have distributors get a group of friends together. They tell the people they have a lady who's going to come and demonstrate eye readings. (My main purpose is to teach herbs, but iridology is the draw. Most people love to have their eyes analyzed and will show up. You will get a better showing than at a Tupperware party.)

When I get there, I sit down with a small portable blackboard. I start by telling about my previous ailments and how I got well. I try to convince them that all the beads in my head are in the right holes. I get them interested. I'll often throw in stories about other people. Then I draw a picture of the iris on the board. I show them the pupil and say something like "I can tell by looking at the size of your pupil if you're run down, under stress, take drugs, have pinworms or are insane."

This usually brings some shrieks and commotion, so I add that I try to be very tactful. Then I draw the stomach area around the eye and mention that this shows the state of the digestion. I then draw the bowel as seen in the iris. This is the big-a-one! This section on the bowel just knocks their noses off. Nobody's bored. I run through everything that real estate Connie and I discovered. I draw lavish pictures of a bowel, lined with pockets and crammed with 40 years of dehydrated and rotten garbage. I mention parasites of all kinds and the vast numbers of people who host them.

I throw in a few true, enthralling worm stories. I do this because I want people's complete attention. Would you sit totally entranced in a class of computers if all the teacher spoke about was numbers? Numbers are serious business, but do they have to be dull? What I'm teaching — iridology and herbs — are very serious subjects and I know it. But, remember, my class probably doesn't know it. I have the power to literally change and save lives with this class. I want my people's attention, and I get it. I get it with humor, because that's what I do best. Here are some riveting tales I tell, which always captivate my audience.

A lady called and asked me to visit her one day. Ordinarily I don't make herb calls, I'm too busy, but there are exceptions. When I arrived, I found one pale old lady with brown curls on top of her gray head. She was hobbling around her small trailer living room. An even paler, white-haired lady, her sister, lay on the couch. She looked like she had been lying there for 25 years. She had arthritis. I think her name was Flora. Her sister, Hazel, had nameless and numerous complaints. They said they'd heard about herbs and wanted to get some.

I gave them my little talk about herbs being food, me not being a doctor and not being able to prescribe, but, historically, certain herbs were used for thus and such. They were a bit impatient at my long spiel. Flora gave her bedcover a little kick and said, "Just bring the damn things over." So I did. Flora took a lot of bowel cleansers and reputed parasite killers, and I can't recall what her sister chose. I thought no more about it, until weeks later when the phone rang. It was Flora.

"I got here," she thundered, "I got here." I was very impressed with her volume, she'd seemed too ill to do more than twitch. The herbs must be doing some good. "I just passed," she hollered, "I just passed, a huge black, oily, red-eyed worm with teeth like spikes! Is this supposed to happen?"

I was very cool, "Oh, of course. All kinds of odd things come out when you're cleansing. What did you do with it?" I asked.

"I flushed the damn thing," she replied.

"Well, gee," I said, "I sure would have liked to bottle him. If you have any more ...." We hung up and I started laughing and rolling. I figured Flora had rocks in her KAZOO. She was having old-lady-senile dreams.

But it was a funny story. I told it to my class (minus names) the next night with much giggling and cutting up. Between droll faces I gave the punch line about the red eyes and pointed teeth.

Leanne, a nurse, broke in and calmly said, "Oh, yes, that's true."

"What?" I yelled.

"Yes," she went on, "I was working for a doctor once. He was out fishing when a lady came racing into the office, crying and screaming. She clutched a bottle of something she'd just passed. In it was a huge black, oily worm with red eyes, jaws and pointed teeth!"

You can bet after that story, everyone in the group I'm teaching is ready to follow me anywhere and do anything I propose. They love stories like that. They practically slobber. If I'm up to it, I tell them *my* worm story.

I'd been taking the herbs for about eight months. Things had sort of settled down and nothing seemed to be happening. I was kind of disappointed and disgruntled. I wondered if this was it. No more action.

Then Keith and I went out for an early dinner. We had reservations. We were just entering the quaint little complex that housed the restaurant, when I realized I needed a bathroom. Keith waited for me in the sunlit corridor.

What should have taken a few minutes, dragged to 10. I couldn't get off the pot. I kept going and going; 15 minutes went by. I could see Keith's shadow under the door as he paced back and forth, back and forth, back and forth. I knew his patience was wearing close to zero. Twenty minutes. Faster pacing and animated pounding on the door. There was an overhead ceiling fan making a metallic racket. I couldn't hear what he was saying, only the frantic pounding and "WHOMMAGUMP! WAISTUMUL! SUEI! BILXI!"

I couldn't yell my predicament. He'd never hear me. I was running with sweat. My clothes stuck to me and I kept sliding off the toilet seat. Whatever was wrong with me? I couldn't get off the darn pot! Twenty-five minutes; 30 minutes. At last, it was over.

Now, when you're taking herbs, you always look to see what incredible thing you might have done. I looked. There was a roundish, whitish-yellowish thing about the size and width of a 50-cent piece. It looked hard. I wanted to save it, but I was in a public restroom, 30 minutes late for dinner, with a wild man pounding and bellowing outside the door. What could I do, fish it out and carry it to dinner? So, I flushed it. When I told Keith what I'd passed, he was so proud of me. I was proud, too. We celebrated at dinner.

About a year later I was telling this tale to a captivated audience when a doctor raised his hand. "It sounds like," he said, "a nematode or the start of a tapeworm." I felt faint and had to sit down. I get a big kick out of other people's worms, but not my own.

The group gathered around me now is generally gasping and demanding to know how people get rid of this terrible mess in their bowels, and can iridology *really* see things like this! The ladies are patting their little pot bellies and looking thunderstruck. "Yes," I say, smoothing my flat stomach, "before I got into herbs, I was standing at the kitchen sink one day. My stepdaughter, Sami, came into the kitchen and snapped, 'Pull your stomach in!' I turned on her, crazed eyed and slack-jawed, 'I am.'"

The ladies cluck sympathy and nod. They've been holding theirs in, too. I continue my talk. "I choose between several herbs for the bowel," I say. "Historically, the herbs in these combos work to pull out all the years of accumulated sludge, bit by bit. At first, as they settle on the top layers and swell, you may become even more bloated. You may have diarrhea or constipation. You may even feel a little nauseous or toot in public."

There are a few titters here, and some shocked expressions. "What'll she say next?" They'd better keep listening.

I do an animated rendition using my hands and chalk, showing how the bowel appears in the iris, and how herbs traditionally work on the impacted bowel. I know everyone is admiring all the pockets and strictures crammed with fecal material; they're happy to know that once it starts coming out, many symptoms disappear, and many people claim they only have to eat one-third of what they used to eat and start losing weight. But, what this group of fascinated folk REALLY wants to know is: What do I do for my worms?

I take pity and refer them to *Herbally, Yours.* Then tell them *I* take black walnut hulls and garlic, sometimes chaparral or a specific herbal combination. I know just how they feel. They'll want a ton of these herbs. So did I, when I first started.

I tell them another story on myself, just as a bonus and because we're having such a good time. I was in the kitchen, when my teenage step-daughter, Sami, breezed in the front door. I heard her exclaim, "Oh, wow, sausage!" She knew we didn't eat pork. I had us all on healthy diets. I guess she figured she and her brothers had all worn me down.

I heard her sniffing, "Sniff. Sniff." From room to room like an intense bloodhound. "Sniff, sniff, sniff, sniff." Coming closer, now, still sniffing. Into the kitchen, nose to the counter, "sniff." Nose to the air, "sniff, sniff." I watched her closely. She didn't normally act like this. "Ummmm," she enthused. "It smells so good. Yummy! Sausage!" She circled the kitchen, looking, searching, sniffing. "Sniff." She aimed toward me, sniffed my stomach and moved upward. "It's *you*." she cried angrily. "You. *You're* the sausage!" She turned and flounced from the room. I guess I had taken too much garlic.

Scribbling more on the blackboard, now, I show various organ placements according to iridology, show inherited weaknesses and explain how they can be strengthened or problems can be prevented with the use of herbs. I often spend quite a bit of time here because after my rousing talk, people are usually fascinated and impressed with iridology. They're ready to take it more seriously and ask penetrating questions.

I then announce that if anyone wants a demonstration of iridology, I'll give them a quick 10-minute reading, no charge. I carefully explain that I don't diagnose or prescribe, and am not a doctor and will not read for disease. I wait patiently as everyone giggles and shoves one another. Who will be first? The brave one steps up, I position him or her and begin a lesson. Generally, the distributor who is hosting the class trots over and writes everything down. I demonstrate on everyone's eyes and answer more questions. Sometimes, I'm even pulled out to analyze cows', horses', cats', dogs', or birds' eyes. Usually, the next day, my distributor announces she got a $300-$500 order. She's happy because she has 20 new, ardent customers to serve and she hopes she'll find several serious distributors from that group.

I'm happy because I had a wonderful time, enthused my distributor and helped build our group. I also know that many people heard — really heard — what I said. The class has been a painless way to be introduced to the incredible science of iridology. Once people see it work, they can become as serious about it as it deserves.

49

DISTRIBUTORS

SIGNING DISTRIBUTORS THE HARD WAY

After joining my company, along with selling lots of herbs, I also signed up countless distributors. Getting distributors is absolutely the easiest part of this business. You simply say, "You know, you should sign up as a distributor. It's only $... and you get everything at my cost. You'd be a fool not to! You also get a magazine from the company every two months and a number that makes you legal." Out of about 300 people I approached this way, maybe two said no.

I was slightly clever, though, I only asked people I wanted in my group. I did not approach people who would only be in it for the bucks. I wanted my group to care about people. If they wanted in it just for the money, I told them, they might as well not start. It's not that kind of business.

After a great while my reasoning improved even more. I stopped automatically selling all the products wholesale. I switched and sold the herbs retail the first time a person ordered from me. If the person came back for more herbs or referred people to me, I supposed they liked herbs and were serious about them. If they seemed right for the business, I'd suggest they sign as distributors.

A couple of years went by. My files began to bulge with distributors. Unfortunately, most of them weren't doing a thing. Some remembered me only when they got sick. I kept thinking, "Something's wrong here. There are so many. I just don't have time to teach all these people as much as I should."

I was giving many classes, but it's easier to pull a frog's molars than to get people to classes. I was knocking myself out, feeling there should be a bigger return. Granted, I was doing extremely well financially, but I just knew there was an easier, better way. A way that was even more lucrative and more fun. I kept remembering my mother's words: "The idea is to work smarter ... not harder."

HOW TO CHOOSE GOOD DISTRIBUTORS

I started listening and nosing about, as I like to do. Eventually, I learned from other organizations, books and people, the idea that there IS an easier, faster and more successful way. I began to choose my distributors even more carefully ... and not so many at once.

I'm not always correct about who will do well in this business. Some folks that I thought would be no-goers have been super-stars. Just the opposite happens, too. A few guidelines that help me single out potential serious distributors are:

- Are they dependable?
- Do they call or come over when they say they will?
- Do they ask me innumerable questions?
- Do they stay (mainly) steadily enthused and not blow hot and cold?
- Do they come to classes and meetings? (If they don't, you know they don't take their job seriously, no matter what they say.)
- Do they use the product?
- Are they anxious to learn all phases of the business? Enthusiasm without the more stable qualities can often mean a big zero.

HOW TO FIND SERIOUS DISTRIBUTORS

New people and potential serious distributors are everywhere. Everyone is a prospect.

Get a piece of paper. Number your paper from 1 to 15 or 20. By each of these numbers, you're going to write names. This is your ACTIVE PROSPECT LIST. Keep it current. Cross out anyone who rebuffs you and add another name. For prospect sources: look to certain groups that already like and appreciate herbs. Some cultures have a long history of herb use. (That's just about everyone who isn't a white Protestant caucasian from the United States!) Mexicans, Indians, certain religious groups and people from other countries are very receptive to herbs and usually have large followings of relatives and friends. (A friend wrote my mother from Yugoslavia, "Venus would be out of a job here. Everyone knows about herbs and how to use them.")

Do you belong to any clubs? Where do you work? How about your spouse? Church? How many people do you have access to in these places?

Maybe you have customers for your herb business already? They're happy and know your products work; wouldn't some of them be potential distributors? Customers will also refer people to you ... more prospects. How about all classmates, former and new neighbors, landlords, tenants, teachers, repair people, kids' friends' parents, your milkman and the meter reader.

Focus on people who are unhappy with their lives or work, those with health problems or those who are unorthodox thinkers.

HOW TO APPROACH
POTENTIAL SERIOUS DISTRIBUTORS

Here's part of a desperate letter from one of my distributors, Molly: "... and I'd like to ask you HOW you made such a successful business out of selling herbs? I must know all the people in the world who don't believe in herbs and it's not my nature to talk someone into believing in them. I must know the wrong people, or I'm just not able to convince them of herbs because I don't know as much as I should ...."

Like Molly, sometimes my other distributors feel frantic. People don't seem to hear them.

Realize this: Reality is different for each person. Everyone has their own belief system. They see their world and everything in it, according to their past experiences. Most people have been taught to believe in authority. What the government says, or the church says, or the school says or society says is RIGHT. That's it. That's how things are. We've all been brought up on white bread and cupcakes, aspirin and cough syrup. Very few people have the strength or even desire to examine their beliefs. Very few will look into their own heads to rearrange and sort what they feel is True, from Lies that pass as Truth.

You will meet many people who live by someone else's rules. They don't know they're not living free. They don't realize they are eating white bread and canned peas only because someone else is making a profit off those products. They think it's good for them. They think aspirin is wonderful, too. The TV says so, doctors say so, mother says so. They don't know that in 1935 scientists tried to ban aspirin because it was suspected as causing heart disease. Someone is now making big money from aspirin by convincing people it is good stuff. "Aspirin is good for you" is now almost a holy law.

Think about all the things you believe in. Are you sure they're true? "Everyone" says they are ... but are they?

By using herbs, you have expanded your thinking. You're thinking for yourself. Many people you approach are not yet thinking their own thoughts. This is why *education* is so important. If you feel the people you approach are negative toward you and your product, look within. How do YOU REALLY FEEL about herbs? Do you totally believe in them? Well, mostly? If kick came to scratch would you take an herb or an aspirin? You, too, have a backlog of old medical indoctrination.

There's a man in our group who could be top of the heap. He has a natural business ability and could sell a parrot a suitcase and a pair of pants. He has seen the herbs and related products perform wonderful deeds. He should be one of my Super Stars. He thinks so, too. Yet, he isn't and can't figure why. I have told him why. He hasn't heard me. It's his negative attitude.

He doesn't fully believe the herbs can do what Mother Nature says they can do. He doesn't spend a piece of every day reading about herbs. If he did, he'd become convinced. He also makes fun of his distributors and his customers. When he talks to me, he always has a negative jab for some aspect of their character or actions. Why doesn't he see their good points, their intelligence, their compassion or their need? He complains about how poorly his herb business is going and ALWAYS has a reason why. The reason is rarely his fault, but, if it is, there is always a jolly good reason WHY it's his fault.

I've been quite frank with Phil because he honestly wants to make good in this business. Frankness hasn't helped. Phil can't see that his beliefs and attitudes are attracting the same kind of people to him. His deep thoughts are being reflected back to him.

Clean your thoughts. Change your actions. Your business will show you if you have succeeded.

To answer Molly's question about HOW I overcame resistance and negativity in others: I'm successful because I don't talk SELLING; I talk TEACHING. And I never hear the word "no" or "herbs don't work" or "I'm going to have that operation" or "herbs will kill you" or "my doctor says, 'STAY AWAY FROM THOSE HERBS.'" I just absently scratch my leg, look over at the wall and go on with my herbal success stories.

With every negative response, I agree with the person! "Oh, yes?" I say. "Your ulcers are bad and you're going to get that operation, no matter what? Great. That's a great idea. You should do that! But while you're waiting, why not try something simple that has worked for some people." Then, I mutter to myself, "Gee, I knew of a man who tried to kill himself with cayenne pepper and instead he said it cured his ulcers!"

Or I respond to another statement about, let's say, a leg removal: "Yep. A lot of doctors are against herbs. I think you should do what your doctor says." To myself I may think, "So you expect to be better off with one leg missing?" Then, I'll sigh and artfully rearrange the cuff of my jeans. "I knew a lady who was supposed to lose her leg because of diabetes. She used white oak bark and she's still got her leg. She's mean, though, it didn't help her disposition."

It's a trick I learned when teaching grade school. Kids were always shrieking up to me, "I hurt my knee!" or "Johnny hit me, hard!" or "The ball hit me in the head!" The tears would gush, blood would run and I'd carefully examine each injury.

"Boy," I'd say admiringly. "That's great! That's wonderful. I'm so happy for you!" The crying would stop instantly. I'd get shocked and bewildered looks. The kids would forget their agony and trot away.

I use a similar technique now. Agreeing, yet continuing on, seems to startle people into doing some fair listening. With most doubters and deniers, I rarely give up. I keep educating them whenever I see them. Always. I do it for humanity's sake, not for the business. However, I don't want distributors like these people. When I DO spot a potential serious distributor (and they *are* out there — lots of them), I not only give them herb stories, I give them the multi-level marketing plan, in brief at least, and ask if they would like to be earning $800 to $1,500 a month in six months to a year or would like to retire in one to three years. If you have to beg someone to listen to your story or join your group, don't bother with them. You will have to continually coax that person to work.

Once you have gotten someone interested in your business, if you can't lay everything out right there, set an appointment to call or to see them. If the person doesn't show or call at the agreed time, forget them. Remember, when hunting for new people, you can approach anyone. Try the grocery store routine. Fit it to the situation.

I know of a man who supposedly walks up to total strangers and says, "Would you like to earn $800 to $1,500 a month in six months time or retire in one to three years?" Then, HE WALKS AWAY. If the people follow after him, begging for more information, he figures they're serious and spends time with them. I have developed a lot of nerve, but not that much. Yet.

Many other people observe the "Three-Foot Rule." They talk herbs to anyone who gets within three feet of them.

THOSE "PROBLEM" DISTRIBUTORS

I've had many people come to me that I didn't like, at first. I found all kinds of fault with them and made judgments, but the more I knew them, the more I appreciated their uniqueness. Now, I can truly say, there is no one in my group whom I don't love.

Of course, I DID get rid of one distributor. Elma. Elma was a tubby lady about 50 years old. She had pale brown hair, blanched skin and wore shoes with shoelaces. She appeared at my door and told me she wanted to sign up. Right away, I knew it would be a mistake. She watched life through suspicious eyes. I also began to suspect she wasn't quite smart.

While filling out the distributor form, she shot scores of questions: "What are you getting off me? What are you going to do with my sign-up fee? Keep it, yourself? Why does the form say this? How much money do I get off? I can get more off at the health food store!"

Patiently, I explained all misconceptions. Then we launched into the bare bones of the paperwork, the marketing plan and a few other necessary bits of distributor knowledge. Elma tried to trip me at every turn. She let me know I was trying to take advantage of her and she knew it. A large part of her problem may have been that she couldn't remember two words past the last sentence. You can imagine what happened when I tried to explain the bonus plan! She thought she should get more money than that and was furious that I would make money off her!

This type of scenario repeated itself over and over again, everytime she appeared to buy some products. When she wasn't physically with me, she would call to tell me about the "better deals" she could get at the health food store, from other herb companies or from people she knew. More than once, I offered to cancel her out of the group and return her sign-up fee. She always demurred.

I kept being tactful, courteous and feeling tremendously annoyed. Finally, I'd had enough. She called one day and told me off, again. At that stage of my business, I was teaching iris analysis, for a donation. Elma had told someone to go and see me. She was now incensed because she had expected me to hand the donation over to her! I thanked her for her call and hung up. I then drew up a refund check and a letter that said I was returning her money as I didn't want anyone in my group who was unhappy. I also added that she was no longer a distributor. In my heart, I added, "And don't you ever come back!" She never has.

Some people *are* a bit hard to deal with, including new distributors. They'll argue with you, make fun, deny or question what you're teaching. Understand that most are simply ignorant, not mean-hearted. They have been brought up to think the way everyone who's normal thinks. They are struggling between old conditioning and new thinking. It's YOUR job to educate them. To open their minds to new ways of thinking. To take responsibility for their own bodies. Never put them down. Just present new ways of looking at things. Make suggestions.

Some distributors take it as a personal affront when the herbs are attacked. They flare back, destroying any chance to open the hostile person's mind. You want to educate people to new ways of doing things. Not alienate them. See yourself as doing Mother Nature's work. Some people are ready and will hear what you're saying. Some will walk away, but that's all right. Meanwhile, while leaving doors open for everyone, continue to concentrate on the serious people in your group.

HOW TO TREAT YOUR
SERIOUS DISTRIBUTORS

When you find serious distributors, do everything you can to help them progress in the business. Show them your special file where you keep all your company's magazines and literature. Have them read your manager's flyers and magazines. These are the privileged materials sent only to managers by the company. Some give recognition to and success stories of different managers. Others contain heady facts like price changes, shipping information to Bunkie, South Dakota, and how to deal with squashed shipments. It's exciting reading because it makes your people feel a part of management. They can feel what it's like to swim with the big fellas.

During my three weeks as a distributor, I devoured Henry's manager materials. I was extremely nosy. I HAD to know every little thing that was going on in that company and that had been going on years back. I practically rolled in all the back issues. Henry used to think I was a radar machine when I went to his place. I'd prance around the room, asking, "What's this? What's this book? Any new flyers?" My head would swing from side to side. "Any new manager magazines?" I was obnoxious. I'd actually get on a stool, stand on tiptoe, nose pointed upward, and check out all Henry's top shelves. He loved it, though. He knew I was a hot one!

Also, give your solid people access to your private herb magazines, newsletters and books. Some of these I loan out with my check-out system. Others, I don't. I let distributors sit and read them.

It's a good idea to have a collection of product tapes and others on goal-setting and motivation. Again, make these available for your strong people. Spend time with your people. Take them out to lunch or dinner. Or, have them over for dinner and a nice evening. Work to entertain them as couples, if they are part of a twosome.

In our group, we sometimes have Super Star women who have husbands who don't understand, don't care or even dislike what their wives are doing. A nice meal or two and some mantalk from Keith will often help make things better. The husband catches fire and a top team is born.

Remember birthdays. Send a nice card and write a personal note. I feel so disappointed when I get a card with no written message. It's a small thing, but means a lot. When one of your group is making you especially proud, call them or send a note.

Here's a very effective tool. When you are in an exotic locale or country (compliments of your company), buy a stack of local postcards, lie down on the seashore's white sand, poolside or in a mountain hollow and write your distributors: "Dear Jane & Tom, Wish you were here with us. You can be. Next time, we'll do this together ...." Then list some of the fabulous sights, the food, the people, whatever. Most of all make your special people feel special. They are. They're your business.

BUILDING
YOUR BUSINESS

Ask your people, "Now that you're a distributor, how do you plan to do business?" You may start by trying a number of things:

1. Direct sales — as explained elsewhere.

2. You can have a profitable business as a *nutritional consultant;* but I found it draining as I'm very sensitive to other people's ailments. Having a tendency to hypochondria, I had to take time off, periodically, to recover from *their* ailments, and it was a strain to constantly monitor myself with "historically," "traditionally" and "if I had that problem," or "Are you with the FDA or CCAB or other like organization and are you taping this conversation?" Then having them fill out a form. You have to constantly watch against prescribing and diagnosing, but many people do extremely well as consultants and love it.

3. Another choice — mine, now — is developing a large group of distributors and managers who are working for me. I spend my time recruiting, training, lecturing and teaching. I use the Multi-Level Marketing method (see chapter on Multi-Level Marketing).

4. There is a fourth choice that works as well if you have the stamina, which is combining number 2 and 3, working as a consultant and building a group through Multi-Level Marketing. I tried that, also, but time and energy are limited commodities. Plunk down in your lawn chair with paper and pencil and ask yourself: "What do I do best? What do I enjoy?" Decide where your talents are.

I picked a few of my managers at random and wrote out why I think they became managers and how they can do even better, by using their natural abilities.

Jackie: Loves people, loves to talk, experienced with cosmetics, totally loyal to herbs and loves her company. Would be best having a store, standing outside, coaxing people inside.

Dickie: Good at counseling, lots of knowledge, loves to help people, knows *many* people. She does nutritional counseling.

Jeanne and Tom: Active church group. Tom says herbs "cured" him, so there is honest enthusiasm. They've been with Fuller Brush, have big background in door-to-door sales and other sales organizations. They're naturals for drumming up their own business.

Lorna: Inquiring mind, knows a lot. Can talk to anyone. She could be exceptional at selling retail, teaching classes and counseling.

Annie: Can talk large groups into signing with her. Should specialize in building a group to work for her, using Multi-Level Marketing.

Bonnie: Knows how to build a group and train them. Good business head — should specialize in training others to work for her.

Louise: Meets many potential distributors through her hair salon. Has a solid business sense, is a good teacher and sets goals. Has common sense and is able to see long-term benefits. A self-motivator, spends her time sponsoring, training and building a group.

Another way I build my business is with a newsletter.

NEWSLETTER

Promise yourself you'll put out a newsletter once a month. One for distributors and one for retail people. I've broken my promise, many times. Right now, I do a newsletter a month for distributors and one for retail every three to four months or whenever I'm motivated to do so.

My newsletter concentrates partly on herb testimonials. People like those. I use real names if given permission. Not everyone wants the public to know about their gum rot and leg scales, but some seem to get a thrill out of being a public figure. You can slant your flyers toward the allergy or cold season; or maybe warn of summer fat in time for people to start bouncing and herbing themselves into teeny bikinis.

Don't forget to credit and mention successful managers and distributors. Do a short column, spotlighting someone in the group who's doing well.

A section of my newsletter is given to Multi-Level Marketing practices or inspirational paragraphs on how to compete with yourself, how to close a sale or get off your rear and do something.

When you talk about your herbs, just remember not to diagnose or prescribe. Use traditionally or historically very liberally. And if you can document your sources (*that* guy said it, not me!), you're in the clear.

I like to put some personal notes in all my flyers. Make everyone feel special because they *are* special.

When doing a flyer, I use a legal size piece of paper, put a heading on it and start typing. You might leave more white space than I do to make it easier to read! When everything is spelled right and all the mistakes are covered over, I take the flyer to my local copy shop and have them run off the number I need. The most disgusting part is stapling them together if there's more than one sheet, folding them up and stapling them again, then addressing them. When your kids are desperate, they may do it for a price. For a long while, I wrote personal notes and addressed them by hand. It was lots nicer for the addressee, but can you imagine how many days I spent writing? I used to do it on my waterbed. A number of times I got seasick.

Now, I use address labels. Go to an office supply and tell them you don't know what you're doing. Can they help? Explain that you want some of those papers you type addresses on, because you want to take it to your copy shop and have them run the sheets off onto those gummed label things. Have the printers run only one sheet each of the addresses, because you're sure to have to change addresses and add new ones by the next month.

Gummed labels make life much easier. Just pull them off the paper and slap them on the flyer.

When my business was smaller, I used stamps. Once I got more than 200 flyers per mailing I got a bulk rate. Now, with the bulk rate, I can't add personal notes, but it sure is cheaper! I went to my local post office and paid a sign-up and yearly fee. About $80, I think. They showed me what to do, and I went home and did it.

Then I brought in my stacks of bundled and stickered mail and they showed me, again, how to do it. I see the same man each time I bring in my bundles. I must say he's very patient. He acts like he thinks I'm good looking, but stupid. He doesn't know you can make a fabulous living and not even know how to sort mail! (Yes, of course, he's taking herbs!)

Backing up a minute ... after typing your flyer, stamp your bulk rate stamp on the front where the stamp should be. Then, run that copy through. (I spent a day handstamping all my flyers before I caught on!) Also, write on the front of your master copy: "Return address correction requested." This means if there's an address change, the post office will give it to you.

You may wonder if spending all this time and money is worthwhile. I think so. You keep your name and the herbs in front of all these people. They can't forget you. You may feel like a fly always buzzing around their heads, but, when they need herbs, what fly do they think of?

I've had a number of surprising calls from my flyers. A man from San Francisco was due to have his testicles snipped off, when he called me. My flyer had somehow found itself to him, a stranger, in his hour of imminent desecration. Here was a desperate man, wondering if herbs could do what doctors couldn't for his infected equipment. Without going into detail, or keeping you in suspense, I'll just tell you that he still speaks in a normal voice.

Many people have called me, a year or two after I've crossed them off my list, and say, "I have your flyer here from last December. I'd like some of that such and such ...." I figure if I get even one nice order off the flyers each month, they have paid for themselves.

Surprisingly, people are beginning to ask me if they can put ads in my flyer and pay me. What do you think I said? "Yes!" Smart girl!

The Herb Line

Hi Everyone. Are you ready for some more testimonials? Some names are changed to protect those already in shock, such as this one:

****

Liz, about 40, has had trouble with her stomach and bowels for years. She's been to lots of doctors ... had all the tests. Nothing shows. She complains that her abdomen swells up — not just bloats — but swells so she thinks she'll explode. She's been taking CASCARA SAGRADA, AND PSYLLIUM HULLS. (She's been so bad, she couldn't even take any builders.) She's been taking them for about eight months, or more, with little result. She called me last week, all excited. "Venus, I kept passing handfulls of things like chopped onions! And I don't eat onions!" We can only speculate on what she's passing, but she finally is finding relief from years of bowel problems.

****

Maude Tinsley is still delighted. She's lost 25 lbs. and 5" off her waist by using the TRAMPOLINE and various HERBS. She swears that when she added our BLACK WALNUT, the fat really started sliding off! (We have CONCENTRATED BLACK WALNUT, too.)

****

Sylvia Stone has a friend who says he's "cured his ulcer in three days!" (his words). He's taking GOLDENSEAL, MYRRH, SLIPPERY ELM & ALOE VERA.

****

Now, this old lady wants to be nameless. She says she had a measle-type rash all over her body. "Big red spots and pimples with yellow running pus. They'd pop open, smell and ooze." She was bathing three to four times a day to get rid of the mess and the odor. Her husband was about ready to get rid of HER, so she took what she had on hand and our historical blood purifier. The outbreak quickly dried up and all is peaceful, now, at home.

****

ETHYL AND PEARL

Ethyl and Pearl are two lovely ladies. I think they told me they're in their 70s. (God help me if I'm wrong.) They've been selling for at least a year and generally top $1,000 + P.V. each month, which makes for a nice bonus + retail. They just love herbs and people. They hang out in a mobile home park where the old folks tend to drop like flies. As far as I can tell, Ethyl and Pearl (both in excellent health and looking far younger than they say they are) trot around the neighborhood wearing herb buttons and reciting wonderous herb tales to anyone who isn't dead, yet. They have had me do meetings for them, come to most of my classes and bring people, and travel a great deal. They've strung herbs and aloe vera juice clear across the U.S. The secret to their continued success is: they PERSIST. And they aren't shy about telling anyone about herbs. If someone isn't interested, that's too bad. Ethyl and Pearl know what's good for them and keep right on talking. It pays off, too. They've helped a lot of people who didn't want to be helped! Ethyl and Pearl, I'm really glad you're in my group. Besides being Super Sales Ladies, you two are so much fun to have around!

MINI-CONVENTION!

This is a smaller version of our regular convention ... for $30! Please fill in the form I've enclosed in this newsletter and plan to attend the one in your area. You will learn many things about herbs and your business and eat VERY well. Bring your distributors. Make sure they sign up for the convention.

****

VENUS ANDRECHT
2220 DIPPON LANE
ESCONDIDO, CA 92027

RETURN ADDRESS CORRECTION REQUESTED

FREE EVENING IRIDOLOGY CLASS
begins Tuesdays, June 22

U.S. goot
Permit
No. 22
m.

cont. page 132

62

HOW TO TRAIN
YOUR NEW DISTRIBUTORS ...
USING MLM*

When I first signed into the herb business, I didn't know the first factual thing about herbs OR the business; but I knew the concept was magnificent. I worked from that. In the first weeks and months, I sold boxes and boxes of herbs through enthusiasm alone. I certainly didn't KNOW anything.

Henry, my sponsor, kept coming over to visit me, bringing his charts and stick figures. He'd sit me down and labor through his marketing presentation. I'd rest on the floor in front of him and try to look wise and intelligent. It seems I was neither. I simply couldn't comprehend his figures: P.V., cost, UPS charges, sales tax, the marketing plan, working three levels down, bonuses at different levels.* They made utterly no sense to me. Sometimes I'd pretend I understood; mostly I just looked worried. Occasionally, I would just beg him to tell me what the heck he was talking about!

I recall, very clearly, the third month I had been in the business. (I had been a manager* for two and a half months and still didn't understand the basics of distributorship.) Henry was at my house. He had run over the entire plan, again, for the 15th time since he'd sponsored me. As usual, he was sweating and I was looking and acting befuddled.

Finally, with a THUMP, Henry dropped the poster of figures down to his feet. "Venus," he said, looking exasperated and disbelieving, "let's just forget this. You're doing a fantastic job without knowing what you're doing, so let's just forget this whole thing." I was sure relieved. I've never liked feeling dim-witted.

I spoke with Henry's wife, Clara, the other day. I was tremendously excited about a new discovery of mine. It's the concept of five serious distributors who teach five serious distributors to three levels down. I demanded to know if Henry knew about this. It was terrific! "Why ... yes," Clara sounded puzzled, "don't you remember the five stick figures and three levels he used to show you?"

I thought a moment, recalling those agonizing hours. "Oh, no," I groaned, "*that's* what it was." I was so embarrassed. It had taken me three years to catch on.

* glossary

MLM

MLM is not picking up people in the supermarket.

It's not going door to door.

MLM is not holding your mother down on the floor with your knee and selling her on the idea of an herb program.

It's not selling at all.

It's educating.

When people are educated to the fact that they need these health products, they'll insist on buying. They will educate their friends, with your help, and their friends will insist and then their friends will insist and so on and that's the Multi-Level Marketing (MLM) concept, three levels down.

From my struggle, this training class was born. Have this as a monthly class for new people or choose a quiet place and sit down with your new serious distributor. Brew a pot of herb tea and plan to be together for two hours or so. Ask them to tape this session or take notes because they will be *teaching this class to their people.* Give them an *outline* of the class for future use.

I start my class by mentioning that we're probably here together because we love herbs and health products and want to help people. I suggest it's a happy extra to make money while doing good deeds. Everyone nods agreeably. "However," I emphasize, "to do good, we have to know how to run a profitable business and it's imperative to know some herb and business basics."

I explain that the herb business can be worked as direct sales, like Tupperware, Avon, pots and pans, etc. I tell the group they can be nutritional consultants or other holistic practitioners and sell the products retail, or they can just plain *convert* people and sell them herbs and products.

Any of these ways are very profitable and emotionally rewarding, but they take an incredible amount of TIME. "After all," I advise them, "you are only one person trying to do it all yourself. There's a great pressure on you, always, to SELL."

The class looks at me, silently. They wonder, "Is she trying to discourage us?"

"Selling herbs is hard work," I tell them. "Many people learn the herb business by selling herbs. However, if they have any sense at all, they soon realize there is a much simpler and more profitable way."

Someone in the class will usually ask, "So how can you sell herbs if you don't sell them?"

I smile serenely and say, "The most successful business people often choose to run their business the MLM way." Most people in my class haven't the faintest idea what MLM is. However, they didn't understand direct sales until a second ago, either.

I explain. Many other successful businesses are run on the MLM concept. Briefly, that's working your group three levels down. MLM and mail order are two of the most profitable and fun ways to make money," I say brightly. "With MLM you are *in business for yourself*, generally from your *home*. Working from your house gives you more *freedom*. You set your own days and hours. You can be with your spouse and kids or Great Uncle Huckleheimer, dig in your vegetable garden or wash your cats."

Most people like this idea. They have visions of lying in bed late and eating chocolate-covered walnuts. "There are also many tax advantages in having a home-based business," I add. "Talk to your tax man about them." (I am aware that direct sales offers these advantages, too, but I'm leading into MLM by sweetening the path. MLM makes all these benefits come more easily and faster.)

I continue, "Another benefit, since you're in business for yourself, you are buying the herbs and health products *wholesale* and getting *bonuses* on top of that. MLM is not *selling*, it's *teaching*. Teaching is infinitely easier than selling. Many prospective distributors will take off screaming if you approach them to *sell* a product. But, *using* a product at wholesale cost and *teaching* about that product? Easy."

The class develops a pensive look that says, "Teaching? Not selling?"

I sit down for a few moments and continue. "With MLM you start in the herb business (or any MLM business) by *signing up with your sponsor*." I attempt to make "How to Start" very clear. Don't ever assume that people always know what you're talking about or understand what you're saying. A lot of times your words will be all mixed up with what they had for breakfast or technicolored pictures of their sex life.

"Then," I semi-shout, "you USE THE PRODUCTS." I run to one of our products, the mini-trampoline, and start bouncing. They have to watch me. Their heads move up and down as though signaling agreement. I repeat, "USE THE PRODUCTS. See if you like them. You should only get involved with herbs or related products if you like and believe in them."

I point to someone in the group. "David, would you want to sell products you didn't even like or use? How good could you be in that kind of business?" Most everyone agrees it wouldn't work out too well.

I then bounce off the trampoline and wag a finger at the class. "Don't worry about making money right away. You *shouldn't* be making money, unless you're selling. And you're not selling. Remember?

You're in this to *teach*. The money will come along after a while. First in little bunches, then in big bunches and bigger ones until you can't figure where to spend it all. But, right now, you're learning your products, taking your herbs and probably spending your first month in the bathroom!" That's not really a funny statement, but everyone thinks it is, because that's where they've been the past week.

I continue, "Take the first month to educate yourself. Start *studying*, now. Read books on herbal knowledge. Get a list of herb education books from your sponsor. Your sponsor should make the most basic books available to you. In fact, it's their job to see that you have them. When you have them, *read* them." (I lend some of the books to my people. I keep a sign-out sheet on my door. When something is borrowed, it's signed out with name and date.)

"Go to all herb or related classes your group has or that you can find. Many people in this business swear to their sponsor that they want to be successful. They show great enthusiasm and excitement and make far-reaching plans. Yet, they rarely or never attend classes, If this is you, your sponsor will notice this. They will feel you aren't serious and won't spend time with you." I let this sink in a bit. If there are no questions, I move on.

"Start talking to your friends, relatives and strangers about your product. Don't think of yourself as selling. You are educating. When you are personally getting results with your products, you will be naturally enthusiastic and look healthy. People will want what you have. They will beg you for your products. When they do, you will supply them. At retail if you wish. You will feel good about this because you know your products work and believe in what you're doing 100 percent. If your customer seems serious, explain MLM as it applies to your product and *sign them up*."

I usually get some comments at this time, like, "My friends thinks I'm nuts to take herbs," or, "My sister says I'll never earn any money." or, "My dad says it's all witchcraft and dangerous and herbs could kill me!"

I answer, "Yes, I know. Somewhere during this time you may get some — or lots of — negative feedback about what you're doing. Some people have a tendency to want to see you fail. CLOSE YOUR MIND TO THEM, even if it's someone near and dear."

I shrug my shoulders. Those kinds of people are of no consequence to me. I go on, "When you first start in the herb business, give yourself a month or so to thoroughly learn about MLM, your company's marketing plan, the paperwork, to study your books, go to classes and tentatively SCOUT FOR SOME SERIOUS DISTRIBUTORS. Again, don't worry about making money, yet."

At this point, I advise my people, "Start taking at least five to ten hours a week to build your business, then expect to be earning $700 to $1,500 per month, six months to a year from now, or being able to retire in one to three years!"

Everyone thinks, "Amazing!" Someone pipes up, "How do you sell herbs for gosh sakes and make that kind of money?"

"Easy," I tell them, "all you need to do is find five *serious people* who want to commit themselves to the herb business. This is where the MLM concept comes in."

Now we settle down to business. I get very intent. "Look at it this way: Let's say it's just YOU out there, educating people about herbs. You're working constantly and moving a lot of product. What happens if you want to rest for a day or visit Aunt Woopie in Florida? Your business stops when you stop. And you get tired, don't you? It's tough work to constantly look for new people to counsel or educate. When you find them, you have to recite the same old stories and facts over and over again, until you wish you would never see another potential customer-distributor, again."

I stop, remembering the hundreds of people I talked to before I discovered MLM. I recall my career in real estate. It got to the point where everytime someone approached the office, I thought, "Oh, please, just let them be lost and want directions." I just didn't want to do the same old thing with one more person, one more time.

I come back to reality with relief. I take a thankful breath and continue, "Consider this: You are educating yourself and using the products. Now, look around you. Do you see anyone you could educate to do what you're doing? Draw up a list this week of twenty or more possibilities."

Someone usually shouts, "I don't know twenty people who'd want herbs!"

"Are you sure," I ask. "Maybe your best friend lost fifteen pounds while taking herbs. They're excited and referring people to you. This friend is a potential serious distributor."

Or ask your child's teacher, "Say, do you know anyone who'd like to retire in one to three years?" (Probably the teacher would.) Teachers are potential serious distributors.

Talk to people wherever you find them. Trot them out to lunch, to a coffee shop or speak to them in your own backyard. Mention the herb products you're using. Be enthusiastic. Excited. Tell them about the remarkable results and funny experiences people are having. Whip out a pencil and piece of paper. I grab one to demonstrate. "Look," you say to them, "I'm not only having fun and feeling good; I'm in the process of making an incredibly good living!"

Now draw a big 2 on your paper. Lean toward your person and say, "Let's say you're in the herb business, and you sponsor two *serious people* who love the herbs and want to be financially independent. You teach them everything you know about the herbs, the company and the marketing plan. You take them to herb classes, show them how to do the paperwork and explain MLM. You stick to them like burrs on a sweater. Then you say, 'Okay. Now each of YOU sponsor two people and teach them everything I've taught you.' And they do! Suddenly, you have four people in your group. Four *serious people.* After the four are educated, they in turn teach two each. This gives you eight SOLID DISTRIBUTORS. These eight teach two each and your group has sixteen people. Not sixteen flaky, untrained, gone-tomorrow people, but sixteen Super Stars, all buying products through you."

Ooh. Everyone's eyes widen. "Of course, you help your group all the way downline* — three levels,* at least. But, most of your work goes into your front line — your two original distributors."

I take the concept further. "What happens when you sponsor three people? Three each teach three who, in turn, each teach three and instantly your group has eighty-one solid distributors. Try it with four. Then five. Five is the magic number. Figure the size of your group if you only teach and spend most of your life with five front line people. How about six hundred and twenty-five solid distributors under you, all purchasing products for themselves and friends? Would you rather try and work with six hundred and twenty-five all by yourself, or just five and get infinitely better results?"

A sophisticated type often pops up from the group about this time and says, "Isn't this pyramiding? That's illegal."

So, I say, truthfully, "This is not a pyramid. You don't make money from signing people. You make money off your product volume and downline managers. Your group contains only three levels."

Most people are excited now, by the numbers and the relative ease, so I add, "You may have to sponsor more than five people to get your serious distributors, depending on how well you choose. Give yourself time to train your front line and get at least one line three levels deep. Remember, each of your five will eventually branch off with their groups and become managers. You will constantly get a percentage off them and their people, three levels downline. You never lose the investment you've made in training these people. However, be sure to replace a serious distributor when they break away as a manager."

I tell them the story about one of my managers. Cheri has done a magnificent job of training downline. She has a knack, but just hadn't seemed to grow past the first group she collected. Then I mentioned

* glossary

68

about replacing managers with new serious distributors. Her eyes and mouth turned to circles, "Oooh," she breathed, "I never thought of doing that."

I tell my class, "Just keep working with five, work three levels down and the dollars and the simplicity will amaze you. Okay. You can see it, right?" Yep. Everyone still seems excited. I pull them down a little bit, "Success doesn't happen right away, though."

I repeat, "*You must spend time teaching and educating your five distributors.* You must spend time helping your front line teach their people, three levels down. After you have done this, you can then visit Aunt Woopie in Florida. Move to Florida if you want. Your people will work without you, while you reap the benefits."

There seems to be a pleasant sigh from the group as I finish up. "Again, the first six months, you won't see much return. Take this time to BUILD A SOLID FOUNDATION for your business. By disciplining yourself to approximately six months of learning and teaching, you will be getting close to financial independence."

As a recap, for you, the reader of this book, MLM is teaching people to teach other people to teach other people at least three levels down. With your help all the way. When you have taught your five distributors all you know and they can stand on their own, make them managers and replace them with other serious distributors.

MLM is not pyramiding. A pyramid is illegal. With a pyramid, products are sold to a person with the expectation that they can resell them to someone else and make a fortune. With a pyramid, people pay an excessive amount for the right to have a distributorship and make money by simply recruiting distributors. With MLM you make a percentage on your entire group's volume, nothing for merely recruiting them.

Also with MLM, your percentage return stops after the third level. With my company, the sign-up fee is small, and you don't have to invest a large amount of money in the product. In my company you can buy one bottle at a time if you wish, and there are no hidden charges. When you're looking for a MLM company, beware of pyramids. Choose your company carefully. Check with the Better Business Bureau, your local Consumer Protection Agency or the state attorney general's office.

OUTLINE FOR MLM CLASS

A. Why we're in this class.
  1. Want to help people.
  2. Want to know how to run a profitable business.
B. How our business can work.
  1. Direct sales-retail
  2. MLM
C. Advantages of MLM and our type of business.
  1. In business for yourself.
  2. Working from your home.
  3. Freedom.
  4. Tax advantages.
  5. Wholesale prices and bonuses
  6. Teaching, not selling.
D. How to work your business the MLM way.
  1. Sign up.
  2. Use the products.
  3. Don't try to make money right away.
  4. Go to product classes.
  5. Get a book list relating to your products.
  6. Spend a month or more thoroughly learning MLM, your company's marketing plan, the paperwork and study literature. Go to classes.
  7. Educate friends and relatives about your products.
  8. Supply your products wholesale or retail.
  9. Scout for some serious distributors.
  10. Spend at least five to 10 hours a week building your business.
  11. Close your mind to other's negativity.
  12. Expect to be earning $700 to $1,500 per month in six months or retire in one to three years.
E. How to make your business grow the MLM way.
  1. Find five serious people.
  2. Draw up a list of everyone you know.
  3. Learn how to spot potential serious distributors — friends, neighbors, teachers, etc.

4. Learn how to talk to potential serious people. Take them to tea, to lunch, talk to them wherever you find them.
5. Draw out the five-distributor plan, working three levels down.
6. Teach your people everything you know; teach them to teach three levels deep.
7. Expect to build a solid foundation for six months before getting a return.
F. Recap MLM vs. pyramiding.
   1. Explain differences between MLM and pyramiding.

HOW TO BUILD YOUR
HERB BUSINESS THE MLM WAY
(THE EASY WAY!)

(A flyer that I give new distributors.)

To begin. *Make sure you totally understand MLM (Multi-Level Marketing). Make sure you know the Basic I and Basic II classes.* (These classes cover MLM, our company's marketing plan, how to use various books, how to fill out forms, take orders, close sales, bonuses, P.V., UPS charges, state taxes and suggested reading. Also covered are basic herb programs: fat, elimination and regenerative herbs. Included are the basics of cleansing and building and an overview of all products and their uses.)

Be familiar with:

° *The Outrageous Herb Lady or How To Make a MINT in Sales and Multi-Level Marketing,* by Venus Andrecht.
° Use the herbs and herb products.
° Attend two herb education classes per month.
° Talk with your sponsor — in person is best — at least once a week.
° Constantly read about herbs.
° Read the monthly herb newsletter.
° Teach your serious distributors everything you know about herbs, MLM and your company.

Teach and build your organization three levels deep.

° Think of yourself as doing Mother Nature's work.
° Make the herb business your top priority.
° Search for serious distributors and teach them all you know.
° Teach them to teach others. Your major job is to *teach.*
° You must spend quality time with people on an individual basis. Good distributors are made ONE BY ONE.
° Jesus spent all His time with only 12 disciples. Look what He accomplished. He was a Master MLM Man.
° By working the herb business the MLM way, you multiply yourself and reduce your own hectic pace. You have a more effective and efficient business.

Know that MLM is not an option. You must believe this to have a successful business. This knowledge will get you busy. Everything will depend on your believing that you must go three levels deep to succeed. If you don't believe it, you will find many excuses for not building the herb business.

Rearrange your schedule. Take a sheet of paper and keep track of your schedule for the week. See what is eating up your time. Cut non-essentials. Make time for business. For example: If you work full time, use your evenings and Saturdays for your herb business. Spend lunch times with serious distributors. Set hours that you work your herb business. Stick to them.

Set goals. In one to three years you can retire if you work hard, now. Strive for five serious distributors. (Replace them as they branch out on their own.) Other goals: Maybe you want a motorhome. Or a spa. Extra money. Financial freedom. As goals are met, replace them so you will keep working.

Be constantly aware. Always be looking for the right person. Selection is the key. If you make a mistake here, you will waste *many* valuable hours trying to work with someone who is not ready or desirous of being a serious distributor. Notice your people. Do they come to classes? Do they meet with you? Do they show up on time? Do they call you? Do they ask you questions? Do they keep their promises and have time for you?

Go slowly in selecting a serious distributor. Is this person one of my five? Get a commitment from them. New people often make the best distributors because they are enthusiastic. Also, those who are dissatisfied with their lives the way they are can be potential serious distributors. Those who seek YOU out and want to spend time with you are good prospects.

Set up a casual meeting. Lunch, tea or wherever you happen to be. Share with your prospective serious distributor. Tell them various information you are learning and experiences in your herb business. (True success stories about herbs and people you know are good, also telling about people in your group who are making a good living with their herb business.)

Teach them the basic MLM program.
° Teach three levels deep.
° How to teach your people.
° Things you must do to get started.
° Building the base of your business the first month or so.

Loan the person an MLM book and tape. (See bibliography for book list or do up your own.) Say you will contact or see them in three days. See if they have read the book, listened to the tape. If so, this is a good indication they are really interested and a good prospect. Ask for their decision. Want to be one of your five? Yes or no. If you are convinced they are serious, sign them up. Sell them the basic materials: an MLM book and tape, *Herbally Yours* (or other herb manual), *The Outrageous Herb Lady....,* the distributor package, business cards.

Make sure they understand how to use the books, fill out the forms, the UPS fees, the state taxes. Explain the marketing plan and bonus structure. Give them an herb book list. Supply the books, if necessary. Make sure they understand MLM. Have them read the distributor's manual. You have just taught them the Basic I class. Teach them this class until they understand. Teach them to teach their people.

Make sure they go to the two herb education classes each month. Mine are free, every first and third Thursday at the Philosophical Library in Escondido at 7:30 p.m. You be there, too.

Set up a time — soon — to teach them the Basic II Class. The Basic II Class consists of herb programs that will help them get started: the fat program, building and elimination. You will teach them about half cleansing and half building and show them all the herb products. Bring them to your manager's herb room to show them the setup.

Plan to meet with your people at least once each week in person to motivate, to teach and to inspire. This can be for lunch, coffee-shop meeting or in your home or theirs. Encourage them to bring their good prospects to these meetings. Teach whatever needs to be taught. Tell success stories. Plan more business growth. Brainstorm. Have FUN.

Meetings and classes are part of our job. It's better than 9 to 5. Take your people with you to hear other herb speakers, to conventions, to workshops.

Expose them to other serious and enthusiastic herb and MLM advocates. (Us.)

Help them set realistic goals for their business. (What they want to accomplish.) Have them write their goals on paper.

Keep them going. Pick them up when they fall. When YOU feel down, turn to your sponsor, not your distributors.

Start building their business. Tell your new serious distributors to take four to six weeks to learn MLM and herbs, to study, to use our products.

Cash on the line. Do all your business *cash on the line* and advise your people to do the same.

Keep in close touch with your sponsor.

Keep reminding your people. They much teach *their* distributors what you are teaching them.

Be a friend.

Set a pattern of business conduct your people can follow. If you don't take the herb business seriously, they won't. If you fail, they will probably do the same. They look to you for guidance and instruction. They copy you.

Encourage your distributors to ask questions. (No matter how silly.) If you don't know the answers, say so. Then find the answers.

Don't feel badly about making money. If you don't make money, you can't spend your time working the herb business. Then how many people can you help?

MLM spreads the word and knowledge about herbs much faster and farther than you could do it on your own.

HOW TO TRAIN YOUR
NEW DISTRIBUTORS
IN THE FUNDAMENTALS — BASIC I

Now, I move into the next phase of teaching. Usually the people you are working with will already be inspired. They've heard your amazing herb stories and have some of their own. They're anxious to know all the fundamentals of the business. However, if your recruit(s) is really raw, you might like to teach them Basic II, "Teaching Basic Herb Programs," first — to inspire them.

Brew another pot of herb tea and stretch a bit. If anyone has fallen asleep, give them a poke. People will occasionally fall aleep. This will keep you humble.

WHY ARE YOU IN HERBS?

I start my Basic I class by asking, "Why are you in herbs?" I usually launch into my personal story about how sick I was and how bad I felt. I tell them how Henry and his problem brought me to herbs and good health. I explain that herbs work so well, I was literally forced into selling them, the demand was so great. I explain that I prefer my new position as an herb lady. Before, in real estate, people were always mad at me. I was the "middle man." Buyer and seller could safely trounce me if they thought their deal wasn't going well, or if they found each other annoying, inane or ignorant. Now, everyone tells me how WONDERFUL I am, because the herbs work so well. I like that.

WHAT YOU NEED
TO START YOUR HERB BUSINESS

I say, "Okay, group, this is where we learn all the paperwork. We have to know the figures so we can do this more exciting work."

I hold up what my company calls its DISTRIBUTOR'S KIT. This kit is full of information for the beginner. I pull everything out for the class and methodically explain each item and how to use it. For example, I hold up what we call a distributor's order sheet. I explain that to buy product from their sponsor, every distributor must fill in one of these. I carefully explain that they must put the date where it says "date." I must also have the month, so I can credit them for P.V. (product volume). I must have their name. There's a lot of tittering about this, because it all seems so simple and plain. However, from experience, I know people forget to write their name, date and P.V. Sometimes, they forget to write out what they want or how many. They also forget to pay me! So, we go through this form very carefully, choosing hypothetical products and filling in all the blanks.

I explain COST, which is the wholesale cost of the product or what a distributor pays for the goods. RETAIL is what a customer pays for a product, and P.V. is what I call product volume or a dollar amount that is specified with respect to each product. P.V. figures usually correspond to retail prices in my company. P.V. is added up at the end of the month for credit for distributor's bonuses. Next, I show the class how to add up the P.V. column and the cost column. At this point, I explain *UPS fees* and *state taxes*. My company ships product to me via UPS. At this writing, the company charges me 3% UPS charges on the P.V. amount that I order. I pass this on to my distributors who, in turn, pass it on to theirs or their retail people. We call it, very cleverly, the *UPS shipping fee*.

I then demonstrate how to add up the total P.V. on the order in question and multiply it by .03%. Add the resulting figures to the COST at the bottom of the distributor order form, then check for state tax. Is there any?

In my state, California, there is a 6% state tax on non-food items. Herbs are considered a food, so aren't taxed. However, at this writing, vitamins are taxed. A good rule is: tax anything you wouldn't normally eat. I charge tax on the retail or P.V., not cost.

There may be some question about whether it's a taxable or non-taxable item. When in doubt, call your state Board of Equalization for information. If your state doesn't have a state board, call every government office until you find someone who knows what they're doing and can help you.

If you are a distributor, generally you just pay the tax to (or collect it for) your manager. The manager has a resale number (see manager chapter) and sends the tax money to the state. As a distributor, you don't need to pay the tax directly. As a manager, I'm very careful about always collecting the correct taxes and sending them in. I have no wish to fudge now, only to agonize and worry later.

If you are purchasing any taxable items, take their total and multipy it by .06% (or whatever your state requires). Add the result to your cost column. Now, add everything and write your sponsor a check. They, in turn, will give you the product. Make sure your distributors fill out and give you the same form when they get product from you.

DATE 9-20-82 ACCOUNT NO. 62751-3   PV MONTH Sept.

PURCHASED BY Sallie Jones

ADDRESS 2231 Garland

CITY/STATE Farland, Ca.   ZIP 92031

PHONE (212) 813-9527 SPONS/MGR. B. Barton

PLEASE PRINT

FOR OFFICE USE ONLY

MANAGER USE ONLY

STATUS	QTY	STOCK #	DESCRIPTION	RETAIL	PV	COST
	1		alfalfa	5.30	5.30	3.50
TAX	1		toothpaste	2.40	1.65	1.65
B.O.	1		garlic	5.30	5.30	3.50

✓ SHIPPED
B. O. (back ordered)

TOTAL	13.00	(12.25) PV.	8.65
12.25 x .03 = 36.75 FREIGHT			.37
$ 2.40 x .06 = .1440 SALES TAX (if any)			.14
YOUR CHECK NO. ___ PLEASE REMIT THIS AMOUNT WITH ORDER			9.16

ITEM PS2040   Prices subject to change without notice   Printed in U.S.A

BROCHURES

Next, we identify all the brochures we can get from our company. Flyers on the vitamins, protein powder, trampolines, herbs, natural makeup, etc. We leaf through the RETAIL PRICE flyer and agree that we should put our name and phone number on the back and hand them to our customers. We make a fuss over the company's colored brochure that shows the plant and how the products are processed. We determine to get these into our customer's hands. We look over any brochures that remain and discuss their uses and how to get them.

COST WORKSHEET

Our company has a cost worksheet. It lists the wholesale cost of all our products, retail prices and P.V. credit. I always go through this with my new distributors. I show how it's sectioned off into straight herbs, combinations, bulk herbs, trampolines, make-up, extracts and paper goods. This saves many phone calls to me, like, "Venus, how much does dandelion cost ... or ginseng ... or lipstick."

CALLING CARDS

I show these and explain that they are our business cards with our company name imprinted on them. We fill in our name, phone number and whatever else we want. I remind them that it does us no good to keep them in our pockets.

I generally find the Basic I — Fundamentals class necessary, but pretty dull teaching in spots. I work to bring humor into it. Sometimes I don't work at it, it just happens. Last night, I mistakenly announced to my class that one calling card sold for $1.65, and they darn well better get some! They were all in a paperwork stupor and found that hilarious. When people are trapped in a class that is emphasizing paperwork, with little effort you can make them think you're a true comic. They'll be grateful for any little original comment you think up.

RECEIPT BOOKS

I finish up with the distributor's kit and launch into more exciting topics, like how to write up a retail customer's order. You can use a simple dime-store receipt book. You simply fill in your customer's name and date and write up their order. Be sure to include UPS charges and state taxes. You may continually forget that, like I did, until you realize how much money you're losing. After it's written up, get their money, then give them their product. Make sure they get a copy of the receipt. Simple.

By now, Minnie, one of my regulars, is nodding in her chair. As soon as her head drops, I know it's time to make some noise, ridiculous comments or knock my chair over. Minnie is my barometer. When she goes, the others are close behind. At such times, I like to pretend I have a three-foot ruler. I spend a few moments "banging" it on tables and shouting, "Wake up! Wake up!" For some reason, everyone loves this action.

BOOK LIST

When total attention is restored, I pull out a copy of my book list. This is a list of books that will teach and train us in our particular business. Naturally, I emphasize my book, *The Outrageous Herb Lady*. It shows how to build a profitable business from scratch. I suggest that all distributors make sure their distributors have a copy. A lot of time and teaching will be saved by simply reading this book. Remember: With your distributors, their success is your profit.

Herbally Yours by Penny C. Royal and *Little Herb Encyclopedia* by Jack Ritchason are other books I leaf through. I carefully explain the sections on straight herbs and their historical uses and the chapters that define herbal combinations. I show how to look up physical problems and herbal solutions. Never assume the books are easy and people will figure them out. Often, they won't. A quick orientation will wake their interest and get them started.

MARKETING PLAN

I always explain my company's marketing plan. I hesitate to tell you this, but I've had distributors who've been in my group for more than a year, come up to me and say, "Venus, I've been selling all this stuff and having a real good time, but how am I making money? How does this work, anyway?"

After I'm through yelling, "How did I miss you? Why don't you know this? How could this happen?" I explain that our marketing plan works like this:

Retail sales. Our company has suggested retail prices with mark-up as high as 56%. Distributors and managers may purchase all products at wholesale cost.

P.V. (PRODUCT VOLUME): Various distributor and manager positions are based on P.V. levels. The greater your P.V., the higher your position. The higher your position, the greater your marketing plan benefits. P.V. — personal purchase volume — is used to compute all bonuses and sales commissions. The personal purchase volume is generally the same as retail.

Bonuses. A percentage (for example: 5%-10%-14%-23%-25%) is paid to a distributor or a manager on various earned P.V. amounts more than $100 in any given month. Each manager and distributor is responsible for paying their people their bonuses by the 15th of the following month. Each distributor must save their distributor order receipts to keep track of their P.V., so they can make sure they get their correct bonuses.

I then draw a chart on the board of my company's bonus plan: The class (or single distributor) is excited now. To give them a larger goal to shoot for, I explain how by becoming a manager and having some of their distributors become managers, they can earn more benefits. I show how it's possible to earn 10% and more on each manager's P.V. They like that.

WHAT YOU CAN AIM FOR
IN OUR COMPANY

Here's where I puff up a bit and show off. I mention that through my company, in less than three years, I've won trips for two to Acapulco; Camelback, Arizona; Lake Tahoe; Hawaii; the Ozarks; Utah and Europe. I point out the new car I've won. I run a few steps in place while I mention my jogging outfit and T-shirts, all prizes. I tell them about my company's special medical and dental program. I mention the recognition I've gotten from my company and whisper that I'm semi-famous. I flash copies of my big bonus checks. At this writing, they are usually around $4,000-$4,500 and, sometimes, $5,000+.

People are thunderstruck at this revelation and sometimes disbelieving. (One lady's husband still insists that he knows I'm starving.) I strut a bit, then pull myself together, look my distributors in the eye and say, "You can do this, too. And more. Look at me." They do.

They see a lady with wild orange hair, old jeans and either barefoot or in bedroom slippers. They've seen me interrupt a class when my 10-year-old daughter runs in screaming and crying, a small furry ball in her hand. "My hamster's dead! My hamster's dead!"

They've sat in my herb room as the washer and dryer clank and bounce in imperfect harmony. They may have done business with me while I'm washing dishes and wiping ants off the counters. I fold my arms and repeat. "You all can do exactly what I've done!"

I can almost hear them thinking, "Shoot, I've certainly got more sense than she does. I dress better. I keep my house neater. I understood the marketing and MLM plan in ten minutes. It took *her* three years! I bet I *could* do better. A lot better."

Once people see it *is* possible, I tell them the necessary steps. With my company, to get in on the big action, you need to be a manager. From there, you're eligible for insurance. Winning trips is simply a matter of acquiring a certain amount of specified P.V. With cars, it's a specified amount of P.V. and number of managers in your group. It doesn't take good looks or even super brains to be a winner and a success in your business. You need common sense, goals, persistence and enthusiasm. You must believe in your products. An easy manner and likeable personality helps, too. But, you don't absolutely need even that.

81

I have a manager named Betsy, who came to me from another company. She confided to me that her manager in that group was nothing short of a toad and a tack head. She stood with me one day and spread her arms in a I-can't-understand-it gesture. "I can't bear the man! Everyone in his group feels the same way. No one likes him. He doesn't help his people at all. But, he has tons of managers in his group." She bent her head in thought, then looked up at me, "Maybe, that's why he's so successful. Everyone works hard just so they can get away from the guy!"

DISTRIBUTOR MANUAL

Next, I pull out my last item. Our company's *distributor's manual*. I flap it in front of the group and say, "Now. Everything I've just taught you can be found right in here." The class looks at me. "Yes," I nod my head, "you could have stayed home tonight and read this in ten minutes, but you wouldn't have. I was a manager for months before I ever read it. I kept wondering why I couldn't answer my distributor's questions."

I stop teaching for a moment. We're finished with the details and moving into easy territory. I give the class a big grin and they grin back. I ask for questions. If no one raises their hand, I say, "Now come on, guys. Don't be afraid to look dumb. I'll be happy to go over the 3% and 6% again, and the marketing plan or whatever. I can't believe you understand all this when it took me months and years." Usually, everyone just keeps grinning, very pleased that they understand everything.

SALES

"Okay," I say, "now let's go over how we *find and close a sale.*"
Everyone looks alive, "This," they think, "is the hard part."
I burst that thought with, "EVERYONE IS A PROSPECT." I get a lot of polite but unbelieving looks. "It's true," I say as I hop from my chair, "everyone in the world is a potential customer. Most of them are unhealthy or homely. They need herbs, natural cosmetics and exercise units. And we have the best. People are waiting for you out there!"

Most distributors still look doubtful. "Aren't YOU happy?" I ask. "Aren't you glad someone told you about these products? If you hadn't been helped, most of you wouldn't be here! Potential customers are all around you." I go over different plans for finding people as mentioned in my chapter on distributors. For closing a sale, I cite examples as found in my chapter on selling.

New people usually aren't too sure about their ever being able to sell anyone, anything. Almost invariably they will tell me several months later, "You know, I never planned to work at this business. I just wanted to get my products wholesale. But, people have just forced me into it! They demand that I sell them herbs!"

HOW TO SIGN UP A NEW DISTRIBUTOR

I explain to my class that distributors are simply people who may have been retail customers and are being forced into the business by their friends who want to purchase products, or they may be brand new people. I talk to the class a bit about how to find and sign new distributors as explained in my chapter on distributors.

DISTRIBUTOR'S FORM

Then I show our company's *distributor's form*. This is an agreement between you and your company, stating you have the right to sell its products and are an independent contractor. I tell the class, "Since you're all distributors, you've filled one of these out, but I'll go over it, once again." I make sure everyone knows which copies go to whom.

FLYERS, TAPES, CLASSES, BOOKS

Finishing up the paperwork section, I tell the class about all the herb flyers I have available. I advise them to get a copy of each one and run off copies for their people. I mention any tapes or books that I have for sale or rental and suggest they start collecting the same for their distributors. Last, all the current product and motivational classes and dates are mentioned. I give the class stern looks and say, "I'm counting on you to be there. Remember, classes are part of the job. You're going to be giving your own classes, real soon, so it's a good idea to come and take part!"

Most new distributors look wild-eyed and frenzied at the thought of speaking before a group, but I can tell they love the whole idea. They just don't know it ... yet.

ASK YOUR PEOPLE
TO MAKE A COMMITMENT

Ask your people to make a commitment ... to choose ONE company. Specialize. Impress on them that they will be approached by many other companies to peddle their wares. Advise them *not* to turn into a store for forty-eleven companies. Suggest they *choose one company* and *one product line* and *stick with their choice!* Don't scatter their volume. You might close Basic I by quoting Andrew Carnegie:

> Concentrate your energy, your thought and your capital. Once you have started along a certain line, decide to follow it to the end. Study everything that has been done on earth in your specialty. The wise man puts all his eggs in one basket and watches the basket. If he is a coffee merchant his whole attention is given to coffee; if he is a sugar merchant his whole attention is given to sugar and he leaves the coffee alone ... I have never yet met a man who was successful when he engaged in two different kinds of businesses.

BASIC I CLASS OUTLINE
(with Flip Chart Examples)

A. Why are you in herbs?
   1. Give personal story. Ask for others.
B. Materials you need to start your business.
   1. Distributor kit. Show the items in the kit.
      a. Distributor order sheet. (Demonstrate how to fill this out when buying product from your sponsor. Explain cost, retail, P.V., UPS fees, state taxes.)
      b. Product and company brochures. (Show and explain.)
      c. Retail price flyers.
      d. Calling cards.
      e. Cost worksheets.
C. Other items needed by a distributor.
   1. Customer receipt book.
   2. Book list. (Includes basic books for training. Demonstrate how to use the books.)
D. Explain company marketing plan.
   1. Retail sales, P.V., bonuses, managers.
E. What you can aim for in the company.
   1. Cars, trips, insurance, fulfillment, recognition, etc.
   2. Help your group see they can attain these goals.
F. Distributor's manual.
   1. You can learn everything from this manual.
G. How to find and close a sale.
   1. Refer to chapter on selling.
H. How to sign new distributors.
   1. Refer to chapter on distributors.
   2. "It's only $12.60 and you get everything wholesale."
   3. Demonstrate how to fill out distributor form.
I. Make information available.
   1. Product flyers, tapes, classes, books.
J. Make a commitment to yourself and your company.
   1. "I promise."

HOW TO TRAIN
YOUR NEW DISTRIBUTORS
IN THE FUNDAMENTALS
— BASIC II

This is my fun class. I have people drive for miles just to hear this one. My distributors have spent hours working their new people into a frenzy of anticipation. The people come, convinced that the show will be better than Laurel and Hardy. In black and white, this class will look quite common. Hysteria comes with the stories and testimonials that edge in while the class is being taught. We've taped the class many times and never gotten a tape we feel is clean enough to spread around. You might want to teach the Basic II class as a separate class or fit it in with MLM and Basic I.

Here it is.

SHOW SLIDES ON YOUR WONDERFUL COMPANY

Haul out the slide projector. Keith always puts the slides in upside down first, then he gets them sideways, then backwards and left and right. He always gets a lot of unsolicited laughs, because he's trying so hard. Then, he aims the machine at the wall, and I usually get the company logo emblazoned on my forehead. From there, we do it right.

HAVE FLYERS AVAILABLE ON
WHY YOUR COMPANY IS SUPERIOR
(If you don't know why, find out.)

I wrote up a flyer on my company and its products and why they are so wonderful.

A while ago, Keith went to an herb seminar taught by an Indian medicine man. After class, someone asked him what herbs he would recommend. The medicine man folded his arms and stated, "I'd recommend, and I only use _____." Keith started jumping and clicking his heels because that's OUR company! The medicine man then added that he knows the founding family personally and knows that their herbs are picked and processed according to Indian lore.

This was great news to me because I've been told, for example, that ginseng, to be most potent, should be picked only in October in a certain phase of the moon. I don't know if the Indian's story is accurate or even true, but it's in my flyer as he told it.

I also mention the quality control practiced by my company. I mention that our herbs are quarantined for 72 hours when they come into the plant and are tested and retested many times before they get to us. I spell out the kinds of materials found in other herbs: dirt, hair, bubble gum wrappers, feces, wire, lactose, bacteria and — the most common — raw sewage.

I mention our company's machine that tests herbs for their potency and vitality. I mention that no heat is used to process our herbs, so they *are* still "alive." When ready to be shipped, they are put in preservative-free capsules.

I end the flyer by naming various outstanding guarantees on our products. My flyer runs one page, front and back.

WARM UP THE PERSON OR GROUP

Ask for the group's experiences with herbs. Tell some of yours to loosen them up, and you'll be amazed at the stories that will fall out of their mouths.

One night a lady in our group, Betty, told us about her 80-year-old grandmother. Apparently, grandma lived with the entire family in a mobile home. Betty got into herbs and decided she was going to help grandma.

Grandma had a big constipation problem and was ready for anything. Betty started granny with a well-known herbal bowel cleanser. Six capsules. Nothing happened. She upped it to 12. Still no action. Getting anxious, now, she gave her 20 and added a lot of psyllium for bulk. Granny started complaining. Her abdomen was swelling up. Betty figured granny had 80 years worth of old material in there, and it was just a bit hard to move. She asked her grandmother to trust her and added six cascara sagrada. Still no results.

Now Betty felt desperate and gave it her last shot: 30 bowel cleansers, three heaping tablespoons of psyllium, 12 cascara sagrada, eight alfalfa and six cayenne pepper. Then she waited. The miracle happened. The family was having a dinner party with several other couples when granny excused herself from the table and hot-footed it to the bathroom. Shortly after, there appeared to be an explosion. The resulting noise and stench from 80 years of packed fecal material was so bad that the dinner party broke up and everyone had to abandon the mobile home for the evening!

People never seem to tire of these stories. We get a lot of exciting bowel experiences because bowels are so basic. If 90% of all disease comes from the bowel, it's logical that cleaning must start there. Hence, all the bowel stories.

EXPLAIN CLEANSING, BUILDING

Half cleansing/half building. After we've all shared a few experiences, I explain how I began my herbal program by taking mainly cleansing herbs and what they did for me. Then, I mention that I now follow a formula: I never cleanse more than I build. Although I *can* build more than I cleanse. Generally, I keep my cleansing herbs and building herbs, 50/50.

Go through your products and sort out the cleansers and builders. Next, I teach my people the historical cleansers, builders and transitionals in our herb line. I use a book like *Herbally Yours* for this, running through all the formulas.

AMOUNT OF HERBS YOU TAKE

I explain that I usually take between five to seven herbs or combinations at a time with other liquid or powdered products added. Sometimes I take more, sometimes less.

BASIC NUTRITIONAL PROGRAM
FOR THE AVERAGE PERSON

I tell the class that my herb program goes something like this: I take one or more cleansers, along with one or more builders, plus add in combinations and/or straight herbs, for one major problem.

ELIMINATION PROGRAM

I like to give a fascinating bowel lecture. I draw a large "average" bowel on the board. It's loaded with pockets, diverticuli, strictures, fecal material and parasites.

Women scream and men pale. They love it. Ocassionally someone has to leave the room. This makes it even more interesting.

Channel

Pockets

Worms

Strictures →

According to my reading,[1] there can be 10 to 60 pounds of old dried fecal material in the bowel. It's been there for years. I've seen X-rays of people who have a movement three times a day. These movements are going through an area the size of a pencil. I mention that more than 22 poisons[2] are found in the bowel, so deadly that a pinch by mouth could kill a person. I repeat what two nurses told me. They had been present at bowel operations where doctors had to use hacksaws to cut through the bowel.

Then we talk about worms.[3] Different kinds, sizes and shapes of worms. It's a nice idea to have some bottled parasites to show.[4]

One night I gave a worm talk at the local library. We trotted out all the worm bottles and gave a nice lecture. We thoughtfully passed the specimens around so everyone could take a close look. Toward the end of the evening I happened to glance at Ethel. She's a lovely older lady with blonde hair and a trim figure. She's a distributor and a regular at all my classes. Tonight, however, Ethel seemed a bit cold. Suddenly she stood up, looked cross-eyed and bounded from the room.

I've had people leave my classes before, but, usually, they sneak out. They don't RUN. Later that evening I found a message on my answering machine: "Venus," a voice whispered, "this is Ethel. Do we have herbs for vomiting? Your class made me sick."

She still loves me, though. She now sits through every worm class with ease (and she takes lots of black walnut hulls).

People love to hear true stories about worms and bowels. So tell some. Here's a few more of my favorites.[5]

My daughter, Summer, was taking a bowel cleanser. She was seven at the time. One day she had the most tremendously large bowel movement she had ever seen. She was thrilled. She wanted to put it in a big bottle and save it. I said, "No." She threw a magnificent tantrum while I did a lot of fast talking. Finally, she was convinced that she could always do another one. So. Interesting experiences, but no worms.

One morning, when we were about five months into her bowel program, Summer came flying into my room. "Mom," she shouted, "wake up!"

I started awake. "Waaht?" I managed.

1. Dr. Christopher - Drs. N. Walker-Jensen
2. Discussed in London before the Royal Society of Medicine by 57 of the leading physicians of Britain
3. Burnett. *Colon Cleanse*
4. Collect these from your customers and distributors.
5. See iridology chapter for more.

"Mom! I just passed thousands of fuzzy white balls! Thousands, mom. All through the toilet."

"Wow!" I hollered. This was what I had been waiting for. I leaped out of bed and ran for the stairs. "Let me see them," I said.

Summer looked sorry. "You can't, mom," she said, "I flushed them."

One time I delivered a bag of herbs to a couple who weren't home. I set them on their porch, not realizing they had two puppies. I heard about it later, however. The pups chose a bottle of lower bowel tonic and split the contents. My friends said they never saw dogs go to the bathroom so much. The dogs happened to have an appointment with the vet for shots and de-worming. After the exam, the vet shook his head and said, with reverence, that he had *never* seen pups without worms before.

After you have told your class a few worm stories, you will have their undivided attention. Don't leave them hanging in horror. Mention the foods that historically clean the bowel and have a reputation for destroying parasites: a good herbal bowel cleansing combination, or two, or three. Single herbs, like psyllium, black walnut, cascara sagrada, capsicum and chlorophyll could be mentioned. Explain the historical use of each product. You might also mention that you add in several builders for yourself, and often work on another problem you might have at the same time.

FAT

Everyone thinks they're fat. (Some of them are right.) Mention some fat stories. For example, a rotund lady came to our house a week ago. She was an interior decorator and had come to measure windows and drape fabric swatches. Keith had artfully arranged five hand-painted Italian tiles on the floor so we could match drapes to floor covering. The tiles were loaners, one-of-a-kind, and Keith had paid a $50 deposit and promised his life to make sure they got back in one piece. You can guess what happened. The big lady stepped on one. Sprack! Broke it in four pieces. She screamed and Keith was near tears. What could he do? He told the tile store the truth: "A fat lady stepped on the tile." They thought it was so funny, they didn't charge him. You can bet the fat lady didn't think it was funny! She went on an herbal fat program the next day.

Other people who aren't fat, think they are and want to do something. Fortunately, an anti-fat program also cleanses the body, so people get more than they hope for. Historically speaking, some herbs for fat are: chickweed, fennel, peachbark, hawthorn, black walnut and psyllium. There are a number of combinations, too. Make your class aware of them. Many people have been successful with the mini-trampoline, also.

As your class comes to an end, all your distributors will be overwhelmed and raring to get to work. They will go home determined to clean up their lives ... and everyone else's.

OUTLINE - BASIC II CLASS

A. Show slides on your wonderful company.
B. Have flyers available on why your company is superior.
C. Warm up the person or group.
   1. Tell some of your herb experiences. Ask for theirs.
D. Explain cleansing, building.
   1. Half builders/half cleansers
   2. Go through products and sort out cleansers, builders and in-betweeners (transitionals).
E. Amount of herbs you take.
F. Basic nutritional program for the average person.
G. Elimination program.
   1. Bowel drawing.
   2. Bowel and worms stories.
H. Fat.
   1. Historical herbs for fat.
I. Close the class.

DISCOURAGEMENT

Most of the time I'm up, but I *do* have my down days. I always felt that the best time to write this chapter would be when I was discouraged.

I'm now discouraged. And depressed and tired. I want to quit. I'm tired of selling to people who buy once and never come back. I'm tired of teaching class after class where I often have the same old regular, loyal, persistent people. Sometimes I hardly have any people; sometimes I have none. I'm disgusted with training folks thoroughly and then have them get divorced, move away, lose interest, not care, change sponsorship, decide to sell soap or dresses or just plain die on me. With herb folk, dying doesn't happen too often; but, when it does, it upsets me. A dead herb seller is *not* a good advertisement.

I'm tired of flapping around, being so darn optimistic and persistent. Sometimes I want to quit. I want to just sit back in my easy chair, eat marshmallows, lick my fingers and watch TV. I don't want to take another phone call or hear another problem from another hysterical woman who claims she's passing black worms with pointed teeth.

But, then again, if the phone *isn't* ringing, if people *aren't* calling or stopping by, I run in circles like a wild duck. "What's the matter? Will I ever sell again? Have I been forgotten? Will I go broke? Where have I gone wrong?"

Along with handling my own depressions and upsets, I have to handle those of my people. I always have to appear cheerful and inspiring. The regular "Rah, Rah" girl. But, inspire them I must and inspire them I do.

Sometimes I have more heavy blows in one day than normal. Most days I ignore them. Some days I don't.

Today, for instance:

1. I drop-shipped* an energizer to a distant point. My distributor called and said her customer *will not* pick it up there and is having fits.

2. Another distributor is angry because the company has not answered her three letters yet. What was in the letters? Well, she

* glossary

can't remember, but she's mad.

3. One of my managers is upset because her shipment is late and some of her people want to quit.
4. One of my best distributors was unable to make manager this month and will lose the manager under her. She's depressed.
5. Another excellent distributor has family problems and can't work for a while.
6. Another just told her husband to take a trip — thousands of miles away from her.
7. My shipment is late. Everyone is waiting for their herbs and getting annoyed with me.
8. The dog peed on the new rug.
9. I have a pile of books coming, C.O.D., that I don't think I can pay for.
10. Three checks bounced!
11. I've lost some important papers.
12. My number one distributor — with terrific potential — called me from her home state. I've spent hours on the phone training her, sent her books and tapes and flyers and herbs. She tells me she wants to change groups. I almost take to my bed.
13. To top it, my bank called to tell me I've bounced a $2,500 check. (It was only a bookkeeping error, but it frizzed my hair!)

This is a pretty average day. I've just had my fill of it, that's all.

The interesting thing about me is: Tomorrow I will have forgotten all about today and be revved up for a new day. Or, if I'm still depressed tomorrow, I'll be okay the day after that, or next week. Maybe, it'll even take a month or two, but no matter how low I feel, I keep going. There's a rock in the road? I go around it. I don't quit. I may want to, but I never do. I seem to be wound with an inner spring that keeps me hopping and bouncing and carrying on.

Here's how I work myself out of the mental hard times. As I mentioned earlier, when I first started selling herbs, people *worked* at discouraging me, and they will you, too.

Everyone seems to get tested when they first start in this business. I almost think the universe is seeing how much you really want to help people, because herbs are a sacred thing, not to be taken lightly or abused.

When I first started, along with the harassment from family and friends, I got the bloody wumpkins scared out of me by a few newspaper and magazine articles. I've gotten used to seeing these stories now, but they are written so luridly and convincingly that sometimes as I read them, I'll hear myself gasping for air and whispering, "Oh, my gosh, that's the last herb *I'll* take!" You know the articles

I mean, splashed in bold type: "Girl dies from pennyroyal." "Couple dies from drinking herb tea!"

I've gotten many frantic calls from new distributors and retail people when they see these stories. The printed word is very powerful. For some reason, we all think *anything* that's printed has *got* to be the truth! Well, it isn't.

Look closely at those articles. Read each line. Read between the lines and expect down-right fibbers, mistakes and misrepresentation. I've heard it said that the girl who died drank pennyroyal oil. Not only that, but an *ounce* of it. Supposedly, if you sip even a bit of pennyroyal oil, you vomit it up, so who really knows the true story? And the couple that died drinking herb tea? It was poisonous foxglove that they picked themselves from a field.

I've done a lot of thinking and studying about these newspaper and magazine articles and reports. Here are my conclusions:

There are certain groups that have a vested interest in keeping us poor dumb folk ignorant. If they can't keep us ingorant about alternatives to drugs, they will, at least, keep us scared.   Have you any knowledge of the thousands and thousands of people who are in hospitals for drug (medicine) reactions? Thousands *die* every year from taking legal, prescribed drugs.* Others just suffer. Many reactions are never reported. There is, in fact, a whole class of diseases, called iatrogenic (doctor/treatment induced). If the newspapers reported all damage and death dealt by legal drugs, that's all you would read, everyday — front page, back page and middle pages. I pay scant attention to scare stories. I consider them, in the main, to be just that. Scare stories, planted at intervals, to keep us chickens in line.

When I get low down, flat right-at-the-bottom discouraged, I call or visit my manager, Henry. He's making some neat checks off my volume, so I think I'm entitled to show him a foaming fit, once in a while. I also figure since he got me into this business, he can just jiggle me back into shape. He does.

He stomps and flaps his arms with herbal enthusiasm, plasters and paints me with praise, gives me a good spiritual talk, tells me his past trials in the multi-level selling business, insists I persist and manages to shove energy and excitement back into my deflated business body.

I can be as rotten as I want with Henry. I can cry and yell. I can say I'm going to quit. I can say I'm sorry I ever got in the business. I can complain about how I only work, work, work. I can spell out my failures, whimper about my volume, and throw mud on my distributors, managers and company. Boy! Does it feel good! You can do the same thing, and you should. Your manager is here to take care of

* National Health Federation Publications

96

you and make you feel better. They've been through it all, felt everything you're feeling. So, use them.

But, for heaven's sake, *never, never* complain to your distributors or managers down line. They might *believe* you! They look up to you for help, advice and enthusiasm. If they see you roll on the floor and kick, they might decide they're into a bad thing. Your job is to *encourage* them, not *discourage* them.

I always like to tell my people some of the trials I go through, so they'll know I have problems, too, and just persist anyway. But, I'm not a constant whiner, complainer or doomsdayer. I don't knock my product or my company. I don't breed and fester unrest in the ranks. And, too, when I feel bad, I just keep working until the bad goes away.

Sales and MLM will show you what kind of person you are, right down to the core. You may be batted, headdown, 50 times in a row. If you spring up and go on, you know you're a very special creature. One who will rise to the top in any field you enter.

Since I've been selling, training and building my business, I've become quite impressed with myself. I respect me. I've discovered that I'm very strong and quite tough. I get hard blows, daily. Nothing rocks the steel band inside me. I swing with the wind, but always with my head pointed toward my goals. I persist long after others have given up. I make commitments to myself, and I keep them.

Look at yourself. What do you see? What do you want to see? Well, then do it.

GOALS

Speaking of goals, do you know most people don't have goals? They just drift through life letting whatever comes, come. They don't realize, yet, that our thoughts create our reality. If you sit all day and think about how miserable you are, that you're broke, that you have the flu, that you have a crummy eight-to-five job in a stuffy office or if you continually think about how unfair life is and blame your circumstances and personality traits on your parents, boss, spouse, my dear, you are going to stay right where you are. In fact, conditions will certainly worsen.

The world is filled with sun and flowering meadows, but you will forever sit in a cave. People remark to me that I always get everything I want. That's almost right. I do it by hard work. It isn't handed to me. I run an endless competition with myself. I never, ever, compare myself to another, or how well someone else is doing. I always attempt to beat my last month's volume, better my serious distributor count, give better classes, learn more or be more helpful, kind, loving and enthusiastic. I am a hard person to beat. I wear myself out.

It took me years to realize that I have a very powerful mind. So do you. For 30 years I let my mind churn out a force of negative thoughts that physically sickened me. I had many illnesses, some even suspected as being fatal. I was in bed almost more than out. When I *was* out, I was dragging. Of course, the worse I felt, the worse my imaginings became. My personal life was unbearable, too. I continually wore the fake ermine robe of the Heartache Queen. Along with a string of rotten boyfriends, I had my share of no-where jobs.

One that I remember most vividly was working all day in a dark, closed garage. I sat at a rough wooden table, facing a gray-brick wall ... counting *rocks*. For a $1 an hour, eight hours a day, six days a week.

As I was growing up and into adulthood, I kept wondering if I was going to make it through my life. Things looked pretty bleak. Finally, they just got so bad, I couldn't take it anymore. I decided to take my own life in hand and make it what *I* wanted. I finally realized that just flowing with the current battered me against the rocks.

Now, I take days when I appear to be doing nothing. I sit in my lawn chair and stare into space. Thinking. Setting goals. Deciding what I want to accomplish. If the herb business has slowed down, I think of all the ways I can rev it up. With sheets of paper in my hand, I rock back and think. I write everything down. I sit and rock and stare. I may do it all day. I see pictures in my mind of what I'm going to do and how it's going to turn out *and it works*. Business picks up. People start calling. Good things start happening.

Always set goals. Sit down and rewrite goals once a week or whenever you need to do it. My youngest sister, Candy, does this as a matter of course. A few years ago, she and her husband were quite poor, with a new baby. They lived in a tiny rented house that had been quietly crumbling since the 1930s. Candy loathed it. She wanted a home of her own.

She and her husband, Smiley, didn't have a dime between them. That didn't stop Candy. She put some paper on her table and wrote out the kind of house she wanted, down to the last iris in the yard. Then she closed her eyes and drew it with her mind in every detail: An older house with warmth, out in the country, with a brick fireplace, sun in the kitchen, wooden floors, screened porch with a rocking chair and a view of the hills. She also visualized a backyard with nut trees and grape arbors, a garage and a barn on, oh, an acre would be nice. And it would be all theirs. They would *own* it. It would be within their price range — which was practically zero.

Fat chance, you say?

She got it, darlin'. A quaint, little house came up for sale in our hometown. The owner had to sell and leave the state. He was willing to dicker and to arrange financing, and our folks were willing to help. I've since sat many nights and toasted in front of that warm fireplace and made cocoa in that sunny kitchen. Candy even has her nut trees. She says she spent a lot of time thinking that house into her life. We're all impressed.

So, another way to increase your business is to create positive affirmations about what you want to manifest. These positive thoughts will pull positive events into your life. Just be extremely careful how you word your statements and make *sure* you want what you ask for, because it *will* happen.

For example, some years ago, I was looking for the man of my dreams. That blonde knight on a white horse. Remember him? I pictured him in every detail. Strong, beautiful, big, taking care of me, helping me, adoring me, hard working, athletic. I pictured him right down to his straight teeth and the area in which he lived. It took several years of heavy concentration, but, one day, he walked into my life. He was absolutely everything I had asked for, right down to his golden tan. There was only one problem: he was stupid. He was a charming, lovely soul, but he hardly had a brain in his head. I recognized what I had asked for and what I had overlooked. I sat down and laughed. It taught me a good lesson. Now, when I picture events or make positive statements, I'm more careful.

When business is slowing down for me, I might make a statement like this: "The right people come to me and buy the right kinds of herbs and amounts for them, and they get the right results." (This makes sure that people who need herbs find them, are helped by them, and we *both* profit by the sales.)

If I'm feeling poor and driven: "Good things follow and surround me. I live always with abundance and peace." Or, "I'm filled with energy, confidence and magnetism. People who need herbs are drawn to me and all things work for the good of all."

Make up anything that suits you. Then say it at least 40 times as you are starting to sleep at night. Again, 40 times as you are waking. Or, tape it and play it back. Then, say it whenever you think of it during the day. These thoughts settle into your subconscious and start pulling the positive forces to you.

If you're frightened of people and of speaking before them, you might try this: Make a tape recording that says something like, "I know herbs are wonderful. I want to share my knowledge of the herbs with others. I feel very confident and happy about sharing my herb knowledge. I work hard, am cheerful, happy and optimistic. I'm a super good salesperson. My whole life and business career is improving daily, etc." Why not throw in whatever else you want to improve? You might want to add in your goals, "I will sponsor one serious distributor this week and sell $500 worth of herb products."

Make an experiment. Choose an affirmation and repeat it for a month. You'll be surprised and overjoyed at all the opportunities that tumble into your life. Sometimes so much money and so many people are crowding into mine, I feel overwhelmed.

I find myself thinking, "Oh, this is too much. I don't need this much." Sure enough, the flow dwindles back to the place where I'm saying, "Oh, no, business is too slow. I don't have any money! Everything is coming to a halt." Then, I'm working frantically to change my thoughts, having to work harder and just kicking myself for ever thinking I had *too* much or was *too* successful!

It's kind of fun to watch the workings of your mind express itself through your business! Some people are slow to catch onto the idea that your mind controls your environment. Real slow. Are you one of them? Do you insist that you are thinking and doing everything right and yet the same old disasters keep happening to you?

If you really *can't* see the patterns within yourself, I suggest you get some counseling. Talk to someone who will be straight with you and show you how your mind is working. Then, be big enough to hear it and check it out. If you never learn to take the blame for your own mistakes, you will never, ever, progress. You see, "business" is just one way of learning the lessons of the universe.

And, while we're speaking of positive statements and thoughts, there's something you can do to help other people. When folks come to you and buy herbs, they're in all different conditions. Many stumble in with broken legs, carrying 20 tons on a 10-pound frame, with emotional problems or a dreadful "incurable" disease. As they are leaving, I look them straight in the eye and say, "You're going to get well! You are going to feel better and better!" Now, I *didn't* say, "These herbs are going to cure you." *Never* make a claim like that, or hint at it, unless you want your relatives to bring you a lunch basket ... in jail.

I'm telling them the same thing I'd tell them if they NEVER bought an herb. I'd tell them that if I just saw them on the street. When you look someone in the eye and shoot positive thoughts into them, you're doing them a tremendous service. Some inner part of them will respond and grab hold of that thought and work from it. These people, who are sick or fat or tired or sexless, are utterly loaded down with negative thoughts they have given themselves and received from others. "I'm fat," translated from "Oh, say there Marge, you're gaining some weight." Or, "I'm ugly," from "your sister is so pretty." Or, "I'm going to die!" from "you've got six months to live."

You are helping people, you know, by being positive. You are also helping yourself. People like to be around people who are cheerful, optimistic and make them feel good. They'll come back to you. I get lots of comments from my distributors and retail people, like, "When I become a manager, I can still come over and get enthused, can't I?" Or, "Everytime I call, you answer the phone and you sound so HAPPY and glad to hear from me!"

You can live life anyway you want to. You can be miserable and suffer (I've done that), or you can be happy and enjoy yourself.

DISCIPLINE

After you have chosen your line of work and set your goals, you must discipline yourself to accomplish them. One reason there are so few people at the top is most people don't know how to apply the principles of perseverance. I discipline myself. I get up early and work late. My phone starts ringing about 7 a.m. By 8 a.m., I have showered, washed my hair, dressed, made Summer's breakfast, packed her lunch and taken her to school. Sometimes my kitchen is even clean by then. By 8 or 8:30 a.m., I'm doing herb paperwork or making calls. (Occasionally, I even straighten the house!) By 10:30, I'm ready for people.

I work at home so I *can* set my own hours. I can sit in the sun, go grocery shopping or set my phone recorder and go off for the day. (I don't do that very much, however.) Consider your business a *real* business. If you were working for someone else, would you knock off at 10 a.m. and watch the soaps until 2 p.m.? By then, the kids are home and the work day is shot. Decide how many hours per day you will — or can— devote to the business, *then do it*. Will it be 8 to 4 every day? 9 to 5? 10 to 4? 7 to 9:30? Whatever suits you. Just make a commitment to yourself and honor it.

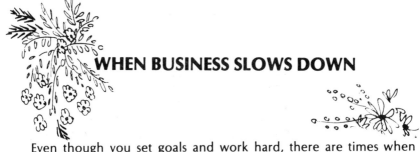

WHEN BUSINESS SLOWS DOWN

Even though you set goals and work hard, there are times when business slows down.

I've been in many sales-related businesses. I've finally realized that sales people follow some kind of unexplainable cyclical pattern. For a day, for days or for weeks, my phone will be jumping off its hook. People will sweep my shelves clean, and I'll miss breakfast, lunch and dinner. I'll begin getting frantic, frothing about how I can't even get to bed without five last-minute, urgent herb calls. Then, WHAM! Nothing. I'll sit in my herb room, waiting and praying for the hordes of folk I just wished away. I'll dial the "time lady" just to hear a human voice and be able to question, "Say, do you have any health problems?"

I spend a lot of time dusting my herb bottles and picking yellow leaves off my plants. I've gotten real good at swinging my desk chair in circles and have learned to click out the "Star Spangled Banner" with my tongue. It takes a true effort to remember that these spells happen. I've just come out of a two-month lull. I can't say I rode it out with total grace and tranquility, but here's how I used it to my advantage.

I did reams of paperwork. When I'm busy, I don't have time for that stuff. The most I do then is make different stacks of papers, often according to color, size, groups of people or whatever whim strikes me. This is *not* the way to handle the business end of your business, but when my distributors and customers are pulling at me frantically, I just toss the paperwork over my shoulder, into drawers or onto my infamous stacks.

Later, when the business appears dead and gone, I decide to use that quiet time profitably. I go through my card file of distributors and retail people, making sure that all information is current, and that everyone has a card. I remove the card of anyone I haven't seen for years, or that I never want to see again. I check the address labels for my newsletters, adding new people and correcting returned addresses. I invent more file folder titles and file all those paper piles.

This is not the most interesting part of my business, but it has to be done, and while I'm doing it I feel useful and busy.

While I'm catching up on the duller end, my mind is constantly running. "*Why* has business slowed down? *What* needs to be changed? Do I need to work more with my distributors and managers? Are herbs boring me? Haven't I been home enough for business? Am I doing too much galavanting? Or, am I not getting out enough and talking herbs enough?" Finally, I grab my notebook and pencil and rush out to my rocking chair and sun-soak for a morning or a day. I may have papers covered with ideas and decisions like these:

1. Teach a free one-day basic iridology class for distributors and customers. Have my distributors who know eyes help me. (Almost everyone wants their eyes read or wants to know how to do it. I'll expect to get lots of people who will end up buying herbs.) After the class, I have calls, for weeks, from mothers who read their family's eyes and think their kids and husband are on the way out of the body. I always calm and reassure them, but, at the same time, this *does* stimulate the herb business. I was the same way. The first time I read Summer's eyes, she immediately went on a horse-sized herb program which she complains about to this day. I remember how I used to have to chase Keith around the house with my light and magnifying glass. He wasn't about to hear any harrowing announcements from me. (I was so determined to read his eyes, I even pried them open and lit them up while he was sleeping.)

2. Teach an iridology class weekly or twice monthly. Show iridology slides, take pictures of pupil's eyes and use them for instruction. Teach about herbs which are historically used for the conditions found. (See bibliography for iridology courses and books.)

3. Give a class on "How to Sell" or "How to Organize Yourself and Your Business" or a series on Motivation and Sales.

4. Change all the classes given now and create new ones.

5. Call *all* my distributors and *all* my retail people to see how they're doing and get re-orders.

6. Write a list of people I think might be interested in herbs and call them or see them. Swallow my reluctance and fear and just do it. Remember, they are too concerned about looking stupid themselves to think I might be.

7. Set up a seminar for my group. Schedule it for a hotel room in town. Call my company to see if it will send people to speak. Ask various knowledgeable people to speak on herbs, iridology and other holistic health disciplines. Have a buffet lunch.

8. Join new clubs, speak for groups. Ask my distributors and retail people to get their friends together and have me talk to them about herbs and iridology.

9. Visit with my distributors and managers. Make it a point to speak to each one a certain number of times per week or month. Maybe they need encouragement, flyers, more incentive to come to classes, more education. Take them out to lunch.
10. *Wish* more business to me.
11. Revise and write out my goals.
12. Take soap and write my goals on the bathroom mirror. Write my goals on cards and tape them where I'll see them, often.
13. Go to my hometown and visit everyone, picking up orders and looking for serious distributors as I go.
14. Read more books on herbs and multi-level selling. Order and play tapes on the same. Program myself.
15. Enthuse myself!
16. Figure a new herb program for myself and try different herb combinations.
17. Ask my people for their herb success stories. Tell others about them.
18. Send newsletters, monthly.

Sometimes I find myself working incredibly hard, just knocking myself out for weeks or even months and nothing shows. I just persist and either suddenly or slowly the good starts to come in, the hard work and effort starts to pay. I just consider through the tough times that I am building my character.

One last piece of advice: When business picks up, *go with it*. Temporarily, forget your schedule and business hours. Get up early, stay up late. Be where the business is, let that phone ring until you're crazy. This is *not* the time to take a vacation or diddle around.

This, too, shall pass. Grab it while it's happening. Remember those inexplicable cycles!

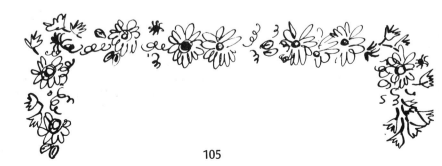

PERSONAL WELL BEING

Don't make yourself sick; it won't look good.

For several years, I never said no! The phone started ringing at 6:30 or 7 a.m. and kept ringing until 10:30 or 11 at night, seven days a week. People would arrive, unannounced, to pick up herbs before 8 a.m., and the doorbell would ring sometimes until 10 and 11 at night. I spent those years tearing around in my bathrobe — upstairs, downstairs, answering the door, answering the phone. Forget breakfast, where's lunch; dinner always late. I had no time to wash clothes, wash dishes, clean the house, have friends, sit in the sun, talk to my daughter or pat my husband's head.

The customers came first. After a while, I lost weight, felt sick, had a constant shattering headache and was very, very angry. Everytime the phone rang I wanted to rip it from the wall. I had become successful and lost myself. I looked at myself — tired, exhausted, no time to just be with me. I looked at Summer — no time to take her anywhere. We hadn't gone to the beach *once* that particular summer. I hadn't the faintest idea what she was doing inside her head. My husband — I wondered if he realized — came second to my business.

My customers. I wondered if they knew how much I hated them for taking over my life and never giving me a moment's peace. I was horrified! I sat down and wrote out my hours: Sunday and Monday - CLOSED; Tuesday through Friday - 10:30 a.m.-5:30 p.m. (this gave me time to get up, do the housework, sit and eat breakfast in silence, and time later to fix a decent dinner). I stayed open Wednesdays until 7 p.m. for the folks who worked, and Saturday - 9 a.m. to noon. The answering machine was on at all other times. I felt immensely better.

My headache left, my daughter was overjoyed and my husband said I'd done the right thing.

I re-arranged the whole house, fixed good meals, became a Girl Scout leader, planted a garden and took up knitting lumpy pot holders and birdcage covers.

Everyone was astounded by my new talents. Hardly a quibble came from my customers and distributors about the hours, but a large commotion came about, "Why didn't you do this sooner?"

Many people set hours. Some distributors and managers work only four days a week from 10 a.m. to 5 p.m. and, by appointment only, on Saturday mornings. If they have other jobs, they work evenings and Saturdays.

I suggest you get an answering machine and leave announcements on it. Announce your hours, class dates or any interesting information. At this exact moment, my machine says, "Hi! Summer's hamster just died. We had to run uptown for a replacement. Be right back. Beep." The callers can leave their questions and orders in return. I recommend this because when people find you can help them, you never have a moment to yourself. It's important to have time for yourself. If you want to help others, you have to keep yourself healthy. Rest and eat properly. It just doesn't give the right image if you're sick or droopy.

HIRED HELP

After I had a chance to sit a few mornings and just watch the sky, I realized how incredibly hard I'd been working. Suddenly all the paperwork I'd been doing seemed just too difficult for me to do any more. I decided I wouldn't. I hired Linda. But I made up an excuse first.

"If I hire Linda, I'll actually be making *more* money," I rationalized, "because now I'll have time to call and see my managers and distributors once a week, at least, more if possible. And I can call all my retail people. I'll get more orders. I can write and mail more newsletters; I can develop and teach more classes. I can get out and socialize and call it 'meeting new prospects.' I can do all the things I'm good at. I can make a buck, instead of fumbling with paperwork everyday."

It turned out to be true.

I'd leave Linda at the adding machine and run off to court prospects wherever I wanted to spend the day. It was a dream life. I could go to the grocery store, smell all the cabbages, run my fingers through the bins of hard shelled nuts, mill around the barbecue chicken ... and call it work. If I talked to the checker or flashed my herb button at the handsome fellow next to soups and gave him my card, I could call it working.

When you finally wise up and hire someone, choose carefully. This person will be "you" when you're not there.

I chose Linda because she can do my paper and bookwork, clean the herb room, stock the shelves, write up orders and wait on people. She also lives right up the street. I can shout out the window, "Linda! I've lost my checkbook and where is my herb order?" She can trot right down the lane and point out to me that I'm sitting on them. She'll also pick Summer up from school and throw out old bags of kitchen trash. She's blonde, pretty and chronically neat. She flies in the door and all my piles of paper and "important stuff" start being magically shifted and sorted and settled into line.

The nap on the carpet seems to stand up straighter and every herb bottle toes itself to the edge of the shelf. She loves setting everything right and making it match. I don't. I like to just sit and watch her. It feels good. She comes in every Friday, for sure, does the paperwork whenever and is on call at other times. She does such a good job, that after she leaves I have to rummage for things to do. The day will come when she may be full time as I plan on having a thriving business that allows me to live my life anyway I choose.

When I hired Linda, she was already my distributor and knew the herb basics. When you're hiring someone to help you, look to your group. You know they *love* herbs and, at least, *like you*. You're not training them right from scratch and they're not a stranger. Working with someone is like being married to them, so wed carefully. If they have a laugh that knocks holes in your head, or can see the bad side of a sunny day, think again. Or, if they're basically unfriendly or obnoxious, think again. Remember, this person is "you" to your group and to your customers. If they scratch their rear, your people may assume you do, too. Firing someone must be as traumatic as a divorce, so marry well the first time.

Consider hiring an older person. With them comes wisdom, maturity, knowledge and security. They generally won't get drunk or run off and get married, and if you keep them full of herbs they won't die on you, either.

If I were looking for a replacement and didn't have one in my group, I'd probably visit some mobile home parks and tack notices on their community bulletin boards. A lot of older folks may be looking for a fun job that adds money to their bank account.

So now you've got some help with your business. What's happening with your house?

I took a look at mine and it was in a filthy uproar. I don't have the talent necessary to keep a house looking good. It *is* a talent. I'm not being condescending. My sister, Candy, keeps her house and children like they lived in storybook land.

There's never any trash, except in the waste basket. No change on the mantel or in jars by the phone. (If I find a penny on the floor, I have to pick it up and put it somewhere close by. "Find a penny, pick it up and all the day you'll have good luck.") There are no "important" papers in Candy's house. My "important" papers are stuffed in books, in drawers or in stacks on the counters and by the living room chair. I might need them. I might need to order an Early Girl cantaloupe package from the seed company, or maybe I'll want 13 orange sweaters from the sale catalog, and, surely someday, I'll need to know how to treat avocado root rot.

Believe me, I *try* to keep my house clean. I pick up and scrub and scour. I shout at the family, "You messers! You expect me to do all the work around here! Are you going to read that paper you just put down? Who spread jam on the floor?" I play the overworked housewife to the hilt. I stomp and stuff, and sweep and scream. When I look behind me where I've cleaned, there's little bits of this, pieces of that; it looks bad. I truly believe you need a special talent.

My sister does all this and does it well. She also bakes edible bread and has tins of homemade cookies. She has mastered every holiday: at Christmas — homemade wreaths, handmade gifts and handmade food. At Valentine's, Easter and Bo Hicks Day, it's the same. And she has kids and works, too, at a "real" job!

I feel inferior, but I finally quit trying to do it all. I hired help. And you may learn a few lessons from me!

The first time, I whipped through the yellow pages and chose the Marvelous Maids. They arrived in a pack — five of them — wearing starched maid's uniforms, frilled pieces on their heads and carrying their own equipment. I was impressed. They flew through my house, were finished in an hour, charged me $50 and did the kind of housecleaning *I* did! And, of course, they didn't do windows, stoves and refrigerators. It took me a month and a half to get up the nerve to cancel them.

Then I fell for a hard-luck story and hired a girl and her sister whom I'd met by chance. They charged $10 an hour and specialized in reading my magazines. They didn't do windows, stoves or refrigerators, either. One of them also ate Mexican clay pots. She'd make special trips to Mexico to get exactly the right ones. She'd put them on the back porch, give them a good whack and eat the pieces. She adored pots. It took me three months to get up the nerve to fire these two.

Now I have Lupe. She's a lovely Mexican lady who calls me "Benus." She's about 40, a single mother with two teenagers and a catalog of troubles.

Her minor troubles are that she has a daughter who's in beauty school and needs a model. I never know how Lupe will look from week to week. One time, I honestly thought that her hair had caught on fire. Sometimes it's stuck to her head and looks like squashed raisins. I've seen her nearly bald and again looking like she's stood in a Texas wind. Most unsettling is to see her sitting quietly beside me in the car, dressed in torn pants, work shirt and tennis shoes and clutching a brown bag of hot tamales. She sits with her hair ratted and blown, quilted and turned under, tucked with rhinestones, shot with gold hair spray and silk flowers flowing down.

Lupe's major troubles are many and varied. They change weekly and make my life look plain. She cleans peoples' houses everyday. She'll scrub toilets and floors, push furniture and *clean windows, stoves and refrigerators*. She often does this physical labor seven to eight hours a day, six days a week, sick or well. I watch her do this at my house. Then I pay her, drive her home and on the way we stop at the grocery store. She goes in, hands over all the money she earned for all day and comes out with one piddly bag of groceries. It breaks my heart.

She's a good lady. Often when she gets home from work, she'll stay up until 2 or 3 a.m., making tons of hot tamales for richer folk. Every cent is spent. She doesn't have a car, so she has to shop close at expensive mini-markets, and she must walk everywhere to pay her bills. She has no money to put in a bank, so she couldn't save money if she had it. She watched her mother die a long death from cancer. She's sure she'll die the same way. She worries constantly.

We've been together several years now, and it's a good relationship. She works hard and is a reliable source of interest.

There are, of course, a few idiosyncrasies. She always leaves the toilet brush in the bowl, forgets to replace window screens and never cleans anything above her head. I complained once about spider webs laced through the lights, tapestried over the ceiling and sliding down the walls. I don't mind a few spiders myself, but they get nervy and start taking over. Then, Keith complains. So, I had to point the webs out to Lupe. She took a broom and got them down all right. However, a lot of our sprayed ceiling came down, too.

She's good about not throwing away "important" papers. She hides them. We have many treasure hunts around here. Summer approves of her because she just stacks and shelves all the tons of junk in her room and doesn't throw anything away. Summer sprayed a Christmas scene on our living room window with "snow." Lupe thoughtfully left it on until St. Patrick's Day. At the same time, we still had Christmas balls on our floors and tables and a wreath on the wall. Lupe figures whatever we want is all right with her. I love Lupe and she loves me.

Her doctor sees her more than he sees his wife. Of course, she takes herbs, but they don't get rid of the emotional upheaval in her life that lies behind the physical problems.

One day I waved goodbye to Lupe, and Linda and I went to look for a file cabinet. We were gone three hours. When we returned, Linda opened the herb room for customers. I went looking for Lupe. I found her, hovering in the hall. She seemed odd. "Lupe," I said, "what's the matter? Are you tired?"

She sprang out of the darkened hallway and clasped her arms around my neck. "Oh, Benus!" she wailed. "Oh, Benus!" She clung to me, sobs shaking her, while I struggled and staggered to remain upright. She's a lot bigger than I am, and a dead hysterical weight is *heavy*. She continued crying and shouting my name.

I was yelling back. "What's wrong, what's wrong?"

"Oh, Benus!" she sobbed, "My children called!" By now we were dancing together in the hall. Lupe was squeezing me and lurching me backwards. I was pushing forward with all my weight to keep us upright, meanwhile feeling panicked myself.

On one of our two steps backward, I noticed Linda and a customer hanging over the stair railing watching us with Orphan Annie eyes. "For heaven's sakes, Lupe," I screamed, "tell me what's wrong!" I had never seen her this emotional.

"My children called," she repeated. "They said the doctor called! I'm going to die of cancer." She unlatched from me and threw her hands over her face, then withdrew them and rolled her eyes heavenward.

I was incredulous. "The doctor told you that over the phone?" I asked, grabbing her arm. "Lupe! What are you talking about?"

Lupe threw herself around me again and shrieked. "I had a Pap smear. They only call you if it's bad news. My kids said the doctor called!"

Oh. I suddenly remembered our morning conversation. She'd had another visit to the doctor and had a Pap test taken a week before. She was worrying and fussing because she hadn't heard the results. I had assured her it was good not to hear. They only called if there was a problem.

"Lupe," I demanded, "give me that man's number."

"No," she pleaded, pushing herself against the wall and sidling away from me. "No! I don't want to know. I couldn't take it!"

"You can't take it *now*," I pointed out. "Look at you. You're a wreck. I have to call. You'll either feel worse or better, and we might as well find out now. You can't go on like this!"

I took a good look at her. She was a wreck. Her face was bright red and puffy. She was bleary-eyed and her dark hair shot out at angles from her head. Her clothes were crumpled and matted with debris. She looked like she'd been rolling under the bed. How long had she been like this? "When did your kids call?" I asked.

"Right after you left," she said.

My gosh, three hours she'd been suffering. "Give me that doctor's phone number," I demanded, and got it.

We careened into the kitchen together. While I dialed the phone, Lupe turned in circles, alternately covering her face with her hands and leaning on the countertop. I'd never seen her act so strangely. I certainly did understand and sympathize with her, however. I'd been scared witless many times by modern medicine and the thought of "incurable" diseases.

The receptionist answered the phone. "I'm calling for Lupe Garcia," I said authoritatively. "It seems her doctor called earlier and needs to speak with her. I'll take the message."

Lupe's mouth and eyes were wide with fear. "Oh," the girl replied, "he didn't call. I did. It's nothing important. Lab results show a slight yeast infection. I thought she might like me to call a prescription to the drug store."

"It's all right, Lupe," I hollered. "You're okay!" I made the high sign. "It's a yeast infection. No cancer! No problem!"

Lupe dropped to the floor, "Mother of God!" she exclaimed.

"Thanks," I said to the puzzled girl and hung up. As I watched Lupe recover, I again thought of all the times I'd been scared to death by the prospect of illness and the results of lab tests. I understood, perfectly.

Lupe was hugely embarrassed. She cried some more and apologized profusely for being hysterical. I reassured her many times and mentioned the comical aspects of the situation. I told her I'd enjoyed the episode. But, as it turned out, not as much as I *would* enjoy it.

Taking a deep breath, Lupe said, "Benus, I was so scared!" Her words wavered to a high pitch. "I thought, 'what will I do, how will I go on? I can't handle this.'" She looked furtively around the room. "Benus, I ... I ... you know what I did?"

No, I didn't know. She lurched toward the cabinet over the stove and flung it open. There sat a whiskey bottle we'd had for years. It was now almost empty. "I drank it," Lupe shrilled. "Oh, Benus, I drank it. I was so scared."

I was astonished. "Lupe," you're drunk! You're totally drunk." I hadn't even smelled it.

"Yes," she whispered, "drunk." She giggled, staggered and looked embarrassed.

I laughed, too. "My gosh," I said, as I pulled the bottle down from the shelf. "How much did you drink?"

"I don't know," she replied.

"Well," I ventured, "was it good?"

"I don't know," she grinned. I started laughing madly. I laughed and laughed. Oh, boy, who could I tell this to?

I took a good look at Lupe. I figured she was through for the day. "Come on," I chuckled, "I'll take you home to recover."

As I helped her out to the car, Keith drove up. "Sweetie," he said in a burst of helpfulness, "I'll take Lupe home."

Lupe and I exchanged looks. "Okay," I said, packing Lupe into the car. I was nearly hysterical as they backed out the drive. Lupe stared pleadingly at me, her face as red and bloated as an oversized pomegranate, eyes bulging. I knew Keith would make polite conversation on the way home, and Lupe would work diligently to make sense.

I'd never fire Lupe. She's too much fun.

Wouldn't it be nice to have a housekeeper? One lady I know of decided she had to have one. She didn't have enough to pay her, but that didn't stop her. She's in sales and simply goes out and sells enough every Monday to pay her housekeeper for the full week.

I dream of having a dear older lady come in everyday at 9 a.m., clean my house, wash my dishes, look after Summer and cook our meals. She knocks off at 5 p.m., and Keith, Summer and I settle down to a table set with crystal and flowers with a grandmotherly meal on our plates. If it sounds good to you, you can have it, you know. You can have most things you put your mind to.

FAMILY
HOW TO WORK WITH
(AROUND) THE FAMILY

When Summer was a baby, I had an in-home, mail-order book business. My ex-husband was gone all day attempting to move real estate, so it fell on me to totally run my business, take care of Summer and do all the expected housework, including shopping, cooking, and even yard and animal tending. You know, all the things that women are driven to do under the title, "housewife."

Running an in-home business with a baby is not easy. There is no way I'd ever slight my baby, so when Summer was awake — and that was often — she was constantly on my hip. I remember those cute ads for plastic baby carriers: "Put your baby in a **Dee-Dee Waddle Carrier** and let her watch you do the dishes." I tried it, but Summer was completely annoyed. She wanted to be next to mom. I could understand that, and I junked the Dee-Dee Waddle Carrier.

When I say Summer was on my hip for two years, I mean it. We did dishes together, planted flowers, cleaned the house (have you ever tried to sweep with one hand?), wrote and typed the business catalog (again, with one hand), answered phones and wrapped packages. It was extremely difficult. Summer came first with me, and I was determined to be an excellent mother; but, boy, I sure did love my business. So, they ran neck and neck for my attention. When Summer infrequently napped, I'd pull out the plugs. Here's where I learned to work fast and efficiently.

I was often tired. You know how babies are; they aren't like normal people. They don't know that nights are for sleeping. I remember late one night, Summer woke up screaming. I was out of bed and in her room in a flash. I turned on the light and picked her up. She seemed okay, just cranky and exasperated. She continued to cry, however. She had one small arm thrown around my back, the other clutched to my chest, her legs straddling my hips. We rocked for a while. I sang and she hollered. I walked her, bounced her, ran around the house with her, offered her food and drink. Still she cried.

Then I remembered her "Binkie." This was her pacifier. She loved it and would spend hours sucking and spinning it around in her mouth. Some people thought that it was a disgusting crutch, but it made one little baby very happy. Mine. I figured she could twirl it until she went to college if she wanted.

I looked through her crib. No Binkie. I looked on the floor and under the crib. Not there either. She must have tossed it from her bed. I got on my hands and knees and circled the room, peering into corners and into piles of baby paraphernalia. Summer clung to her monkey mother and screamed. It was now 3:30 a.m., an hour since I'd gotten up with her.

My husband lay sleeping, easily, in the next room. This just wasn't fair. How could he let me stay up all night like this? How could he just *sleep,* for heaven's sake. I'd be up at 5 a.m. with Summer and I had mountains of work to do. I had a catalog to finish typing, run off and mail out. I had stacks of books to wrap. I had groceries to buy and rooms to clean. I started to cry. Where was that damn Binkie? Where was my damn husband?

I lurched myself off the floor, nearly tumbling both Summer and me, and stormed into my bedroom. "Get up," I commanded. I was shaking with righteousness. "I need help!" Summer's dad rose ball-eyed from the covers. I sniffled and whined, "I'm tired. I'm cold." Summer screamed accompaniment. "I have to work all day tomorrow and you're sleeping. I can't ..." I shrilled, my voice rising, "find her Binkie!"

I stumbled back to Summer's room, my husband trailing behind me. We tore the room apart. Then we searched the rest of the house. By now, it was 4:30 a.m. Summer had stopped crying and was having a wonderful time. She cooed her approval as her father and I threw accusations and insults at each other. Surely it was *my* fault the Binkie was lost, and what made *him* think I should be up all night when I worked too?

The Binkie was not to be found. There was nothing more to do but put Summer to bed and let her yell, if that's what she wanted. We padded into her room; I unhooked her arm from my back and placed her in her crib. With her arm came a Binkie, tightly held in her little fist. I was stupefied. Nonchalantly, she popped it into her mouth and began sucking and twirling, smiling delightedly. Her eyes showed her amusement. All this time, two hours, she had held her Binkie against my back! I didn't even bother to go back to bed. It was almost 5 a.m.

When I began my herb business, I didn't have baby and Binkie problems; but I did have a seven-year-old daughter, a new husband and three teenage step-children who considered me a large intrusion in their lives. I also still had a house and yard to run (with all that goes with it), and I had another fulltime job.

I had to deal with thundering acid-rock music, teenagers and teenagers' friends, insubordination and complaints. Sami, my step-daughter, grumbled bitterly about being awakened early on Saturday mornings by my herb customers and distributors. The herb room and her room shared one wall. She also didn't dare walk out of her room in a nightgown. I could see her point. I also was, several times, mightily embarrassed by tantrums thrown by my oldest stepson in front of my customers.

Before I set hours, it was difficult to keep the house clean and fix dinner. You would think with a house full of large children that some of this would have been done for me. Unfortunately, I found that arriving so late in their lives brought little respect and less help. Trying to build a base of power and yet make them like me, if not love me, also took strength and time. There were a number of times when I complely forgot to fix meals.

I remember one Saturday, Keith drifted up the stairs and into the herb room. He said hello to a passel of old ladies and asked if I minded if he took an herb bar. He let it slip that we hadn't had breakfast or lunch. (Yes, I *hope* he felt embarrassed because he hadn't fixed something. But, if you are a woman with a husband and kids, maybe you can identify with his attitude. I don't think he'd ever had a wife like me before. He hadn't realized, yet, that chores were going to have to be more 50-50.)

Actually, he's been very supportive. He has been instrumental in finding new distributors, has taught classes, and always tells me how great I am.

I know many women in business, though, who have husband troubles. There's Laura. She complains about her husband not "letting" her come to classes. He also controls the checkbook and won't "let" her have any money. He wants, and insists, that she stay home and take care of the house, the kids and him.

I'm not a carded women's libber. I'm a person's libber. I believe that each of us should do what we have to do. I spent years trying to follow the female role as I understood it. I tried to follow it because I was afraid. Afraid a man wouldn't love me. Or I wouldn't get married or stay married. Or be happy. Well, I did get married and I got unmarried, too. Then, I got married, again. Still trying to follow the "rules" for women, I almost got unmarried again. I finally realized that I'm an important human being. I have to live my life the way I know it should be lived. This means, for me, that I spend a great part of my life on my herb business. I work hard to keep my family and husband happy, but not at my expense. If I'm miserable, mean and unfulfilled, they will be, too.

Another girl, Cathy, took an iridology course but was very upset when her husband wouldn't "let" her finish the crucial part of the course. He had pretended to be behind her, but, when knock came to shake, he was afraid she was giving too much time to business. That is, too much time away from him. Get your husband (wife) and kids involved in your business. This will cut out the jealousy and complaints.

Husband-and-wife teams are tremendously successful. There's power in the number two. Your husband (wife) isn't interested? Wear them down. When they see you blooming with health and bringing in *money* (lots of money), you suddenly get their interest and some grudging respect.

I began the herb business on my own, and now Keith is planning to come into it full time with me. I can see us already. Getting up as late as we wish, taking vacations when we want, going out to lunch and seeing movies in the daytime. What freedom!

Often, Summer helps me with the business. I started her out when she was nine, paying her to stock shelves. Stocking my shelves is a tough job. There are lots of products and Summer is a perfectionist. As soon as the boxes would come, Summer would go to work. She'd carefully open each box and extract each bottle. Bottle by bottle, she would place them in position. Six damiana here, six more on top, with 12 dandelion beside them, then add three more dandelion, woops. A bottle would shoot sideways and knock off three rows of herbs. They'd hit the wall with a crash, bounce back and smack two more rows on the way down. There would be a pile on the floor and one frustrated child. She'd put them all back, turn around and her elbow would send another three rows sliding. She'd put them back and add some more. Each bottle had to be perfectly lined and placed. This would go on for hours. I'd look up and see Summer's face becoming pinched and pale, her breathing coming in shallow jerks.

"Knock off work," I'd command. "Take a break."

"No," she'd moan. "I have to finish." More bottles would drop, tears would fall.

"I mean it, Summer," I'd say. "You're wearing yourself out. It doesn't have to be done today, and it doesn't have to be so perfect. Stop working!"

She'd keep on, opening boxes, lining up herbs, breathing fast and turning in frantic circles. I'd finally jump up and push her bodily from the room. Eventually I had to fire her. She just worked too hard. I feel a little guilty wondering what kind of work driven example I've set for her, all these years.

One thing I have promoted is her self-reliance and independence. She's been dressing and looking out for herself since she was two. Hanging onto me for two years solid seemed to fill all her dependency needs. She's extraordinarily creative and always keeps herself amused with ongoing, self-designed projects.

When she was about six, Keith and I left her with my folks for two weeks while we went to Mexico City. I worried about her the entire time. When we returned to the United States and drove to pick her up at grandma's, I kept voicing my concerns to Keith.

"Poor Summer, I remember how terrible I used to feel when my folks went on vacations. I stopped living until they got home. I bet she's miserable. Two weeks is a long time to leave her, Keith." I wallowed a bit in guilt. "I bet she cries when she sees me, she'll be so relieved. Poor baby. I feel just awful!"

As we swung into my folk's country drive, I saw her little blonde head, bobbing around in the bushes. She was carefully collecting peacock feathers. Keith had barely halted the car, when I was out the door, running, arms outstretched to my baby. "Summer, Summer!" She looked at me blankly as I approached.

"Oh, what?" she said.

I tucked her in my arms. "Oh, Summer, are you okay?" She pulled back and looked at me, a finger stuck in her ear. She looked purely puzzled and surprised. "Oh, mom, I forgot all about you," she said.

That's when I stopped feeling guilty about working. Summer capped it a year later when I returned from another trip. This time she didn't want to hurt my feelings. As I cautiously asked her if she'd missed me, she explained, "Well, mom, I've been sooo busy, you know?"

Now, at 10 years, Summer helps me with customers, answers the phone, takes messages and puts together newsletters. She also babysits customers' children, but she does *not* stock shelves. She's had a savings account now for years. She puts every dime and dollar that she earns into it.

When she was seven or eight, I asked her how she was going to use all this money she was saving. She told me, of course, that it's for her car and apartment when she leaves home.

Did you know you can hire and pay your kids up to a certain amount and it's tax deductible?

I know a number of women in this business who get up at 5 a.m. They get their wash done, house cleaned and lunches packed before the family hauls out of bed. This gives them time to work later in the day on the business.

If the kids all trot off to school, you're in easy city. If they don't, you just have to be more ingenious. One mom I know has taken wire and strung it around her desk, her chair and some working space. She locks herself in there and tells her little kid that he can have the rest of the house.

So they can work, other mothers hire a teenager to come in several times a week or more and play with the kids.

If all else fails, develop an attitude like my mother's. There were six of us kids and we could have driven her crazy. She always worked at home, too. Instead, I remember her unusual ability to strictly tune us out. We'd be running circles around the house, hanging from door jambs, beating on each other and writing on the walls with crayons. She'd sit calmly, reading a book. I'd frequently run over and scream, "Jim hit me!" For telling, he'd smack me again. "Whack!" and then, again, "whack!" Polly would jump in and accuse me of starting it and I'd try to rake her with my fingernails. Jim would then smack Polly. Mom would keep her eyes on the book.

Mom could, however, be reached at really important times. I shook her once to tell her that Art had eaten two blue glass Christmas balls. She seemed semi-alarmed, opened his mouth to look and asked if he felt ckay. I think she made him eat some bread.

The fact is: she was a good mother. We all grew up and are now, for some odd reason, superachievers.

What you might do is what I did early on in my work life. I sat down with my paper and pen and wrote out my priorities. Housework was at the bottom of the list. Decide where your priorities are and adjust your time to them.

I've acclimated my family to my work pretty well. It's my cat, Mouser, who needs more togetherness. She and the dog trail me around the house from room to room. Mouser's in the herb room the second the doorbell rings. She likes people. If I have to work at my desk, she's right there on top and in the most important "in" basket, walks me to the mailbox and follows me to the bathroom. And I'm not worried about her growing up sassy or getting into dope. She's already 15 and pretty much developed.

119

SUMMING IT ALL UP

MAIL ORDER AND UPS

Some folks, very well meaning, will say, "Don't get retail people or sign up distributors in other parts of the country. You can't service them, and you can't train them!"

I say, "Maybe that's so." But, I've found that far away people who take the time to call you, to write you and to think enough of you and your product to order from you can be your future managers. And, your Super Stars. Some of the best people I have, I've never met. You can call back and forth when phone rates are low. You can educate them right over the phone. I've done many long distance bowel and worm lectures. I've taken people right from zero, taught them over the phone and mailed them flyers, tapes and books. Truly, these people who are self-motivators are excellent. Don't overlook or give them away.

But, beware. Everyone may not be as honest as you are. I try to find someone working with my company — in my distributor's area — to help them out. In return, I do whatever I can to help the person who helps them. However, here's where you may run into problems. Sometimes the person helping them entices them to their group. You can understand how that might happen. It's not a package of fun for a manager to work with someone they know will never benefit them. And it's easier for a distributor to be with a group that is close by.

One of my best managers is Melissa, a lady I met for an hour. She was passing through California from Michigan. She came to a lecture of mine and later came to my house. We talked, briefly. I signed her up, and she bought a sack of herbs. I, shamefully, never called to check on her. I figured, "Goodbye, she's gone."

She called ME, several months later, trembling with excitement. She'd lost weight, her skin had cleared up, and she felt tremendous. She wanted to be a manager, right away. Suddenly, *I* felt tremendous. I worked with Melissa by phone and letter, but she did most of it on her own. Like most of us, she started by knowing nothing and forged ahead, anyway.

When her group expanded a bit, her distributors and retail people chipped in $5 to $10 each to fly me back to Michigan. I spent four to five days teaching classes. By the time I left, Melissa had herb orders for at least $3,500. It was simply a matter of herb education and enthusiasm.

It's easy to get products to your people in other areas. For a small fee, UPS* comes to my door each weekday and carts off my packages. It's quite economical for your people, too. You can even ship C.O.D.*, so you'll be sure to get your money. Also, delivery is very fast, and that's what your people want. Be prompt with mailouts. Fast service is one more reason your people will stick with you. Call your local UPS and set up the procedure.

As your newsletter expands and spreads, you'll also find you're doing more mail order business. Total strangers will read your fascinating articles and say, "I want some of those herbs." And you've got an order.

For packaging, you can get boxes from your company, local stores or look in the yellow pages under "Packaging" for the materials you need for mail order.

The UPS man also gives my old dog something to live for. Russell, a scruffy red doxie, lies in wait for that poor man every afternoon. He careens after him, nipping at his heels, getting underfoot and yapping frantically. No one excites him like UPS. (Make sure you get your UPS, freight delivery and mail persons all hooked on herbs. Never let an opportunity go by.)

I like mail order. I love to get orders, letters and checks in the mail. I always hope for love letters, but I satisfy myself with checks.

CHOOSE THE RIGHT COMPANY AND STICK WITH THEM

Once you've chosen your company and product, *stick with them.* Many people will approach you to sell their goods — especially as you get more and more successful — but stay with one company. You may find many excellent companies and products, but why do you have to market them? If I like a different product, I tell people where to get it. LOYALTY makes sense. It's good for the company you represent, and it's good for you. See it this way:

You've chosen your company because you like its products, its marketing plan and its people. You've set a goal. You want to climb to the top, or at least make it to the point where you are in on the real action: winning new cars, earning trips, making big bonuses, getting extras, receiving recognition and making lots of money. Why would you want to divert your newly concentrated energy into someone else's product and marketing plan? Why would you want to split

* glossary

121

yourself once or twice or thrice or more?

There was a man in my company who was very BIG. He was making an exceedingly good living. When I first met this man, he was in the process of buying an enormous ranch, a gorgeous mansion and another new car. He was also in the process of signing up with, and distributing, several other lines of products. At this point, my acquaintance has gone from a Blazing Company Star to a dimly smouldering meteorite. This person is no longer a star in *any* of the companies. And, can you guess what's happened to the volume and bonus checks?

Sometimes people do this because they're truly entranced by the other products and think they *have* to supply this to their people. It's too good to let it go by. That's a noble thought, but why go broke over it? Why not tell your people where they can buy it? You might lose business? Nonsense. There is no competition. If you refer people to other distributors, they'll refer people to you.

People will keep coming to you because they like you and believe in what you have to offer. Also, any good you do comes back to you. Or, don't you really believe that?

Why else do people split themselves up? They're greedy. They think the new marketing plan is fabulous, and, if they sell the product, they'll make extra money. Maybe LOTS of money. But, they overlook the fact that as their volume goes down with their original company, so do their bonus checks. And, how can their volume help but go down if they're selling competing products? They're scattering their energies like someone who's promiscuous. If you are selling this product and that product, how do you stay tops in any ONE company? Or, do you become mediocre in all?

And how about all the people in your group who depend on you and look to you for guidance? Pretty soon you have a disorganized passel of people under you, all signed up in different groups, doing different things. What's happened to your volume then?

Aside from the money loss, have you considered the paperwork involved? You have to keep all these distributors straight; who is signed up where; who gets what money; who ordered what; who's under who. And you are going to have to buy a lot more stock, kids. And store it, somewhere, too. Also, to do a good job with your new investments, you've got to learn about each company, in depth. How can you sell something you don't understand. And how are you going to teach all your people about these new products, new marketing plans, new paperwork? I've gotten confused just writing about how confusing this can be. You'll be mucking around in all this, when you should be busy marketing your original line and building a good, strong one-pointed, three-leveled group under you.

I do suggest, however, that you keep your mind open. When someone hustles you for a "fabulous opportunity, you've got to check this out. You've got to sign up!" (They are *always* fabulous opportunities, and, if you pass them up, you are *always* losing the chance of a lifetime.) Check it out.

I sometimes buy a few of the products and test them on myself or semi-willing family members. The latest was "Fabulous Wrinkle Rot" guaranteed, by implication, to return your face to that of a six year old. Months later, my mother is still faithfully testing "Wrinkle Rot" for me, with no discernable results. Unless, that is, you count the man who turned to her one day and said, "My, you must have been beautiful when you were young."

I will travel almost anywhere to hear a new marketing plan, to see how a product is presented, to watch how the leader hypes the group and to hear all his sales suggestions. Heck, why not? I'm learning a lot. Much that will help me inspire and strengthen MY group. I've sat through many presentations, laughed inwardly at the line that's being promoted as the new "wonderkins," that'll make us all rich and blessed. I've also gotten so excited by some that I'm ready to quit everything I've built up and follow the new leader, anywhere.

Then, I go home and think about it. I get logical and unemotional. Sometimes I decide the new products are great, but not enough money in them. Or, fabulous money, but I would have to sell my soul to make it. Or, it's okay, but why bother? Or, I'm impressed, I'll recommend it. Many times I see it for what it is: a flash in the pan. No star I'd want to follow.

There are many, many multi-level selling plans now and more to come. How many do you think will be here next year ... and the next? Ask someone who's been in multi-level selling a LONG time, "How many of these companies go under, and how soon?" They will tell you about all the hot companies that have burned bright, then fizzled out. Be smart. Choose wisely, well and STICK TO YOUR CHOICE.

MY LIFE NOW

It's been a bit more than two years since I seriously started working my business. My business and I have been through a lot, together. It's grown and I've grown. I'm a different person from when I started.

I've developed a lot of respect for myself. I figure I began with a bottle of herbs and built a large business that now supports my family. I looked at every obstacle — and there were many — and said, "Ha, you won't stop me," and went around them. I taught myself business skills I never had before. I've become strong inside. I think my own thoughts, say what I think and stand up to opposition. I feel independent. My marriage has improved and so has my husband. He's been able to leave a job he detested and a life he had outgrown. He's a healthier, happier man. I know, for sure, that forever after, I can always support and take care of myself. It's a heady feeling. I feel I'm on an even footing with everyone and I KNOW I can do or have anything I want out of life. It only takes work and will. And, so, as we come to the end of this chapter of my life, I hope that my accomplishments may be a springboard for a new, profitable and happy beginning for you.

Much love,

Venus

To contact Venus
   write:
   % Ransom Hill Press
   P.O. Box 325
   Ramona, CA 92065

GLOSSARY

Bonus A dollar percentage earned on your monthly purchase volume (P.V.).

Bulk rate A lower postal rate given on mass mailings. Check with your post office for details.

C.O.D. A person can ship a product to others via UPS or the post office and specify that a check or cash be collected from the receiver. This is a smart way to do business.

Direct sales Items are sold retail, directly to customers. Encyclopedias, Avon, Tupperware, life insurance, etc. are examples. A person works at directly selling for the company and doesn't build an organization. When moving, the built-up business is left behind.

Distributor As an independent contractor with a particular company you are able to obtain all company products at cost and sell at retail and are allowed to sponsor and train other distributors under you and build an organization.

Downline Any people in your group who signed as distributors directly under you, under your distributors or under your distributors' distributors, etc. For example: you are the great grandma. Your downline is the grandmother ... mother ... daughter. Having a group downline is like having a pile of children, some of which you can't even recall giving birth to.

Downline managers Let's say you sponsored Carl who popped away as one of your frontline (downline) managers. He, in turn, made Ellie (one of his distributors) a manager and eventually she made one of her distributors a manager. You have a line three levels deep.

Dropship With my company, when you're a manager, you can dropship product to distant points. You send your order to the company (it must be at least $50 P.V.) with a small dropship fee and a filled out dropship form, and the company will ship the product directly to your customer.

Historically "Historically, garlic prevents colds." If anyone who is dead said certain herbs work for certain diseases, you can say it, too. Safely. People who are dead have credibility.

Independent contractors Persons who are self-employed, make their own hours, have own place of business and are responsible for themselves. Get supplies from you or from the company.

Manager Someone who is "big time" in the business. You now buy your product directly from the company, must keep up a certain volume and have more paperwork. You also make more money.

Marketing plan Study this plan closely. It shows if you can make a living with the company you have chosen. The plan tells you what levels you and your group can attain and the dollar percentages.

MLM With Multi-Level Marketing you *teach* people about your product. You don't *sell* it. They buy it because they now know why they want it. You sponsor and train people three levels down to educate and build their business.

P.V. Product volume. P.V. usually corresponds to retail prices. Different companies may have different names for product volume.

Pyramiding This is illegal. It's a marketing plan built from the top down. Only those in at the very beginning can ever be at the top.

Retail The mark-up price from cost.

Serious distributors The distributors who sincerely want to build a business, make a good living and help people.

Sponsor A sponsor signs up distributors and teaches them everything he/she knows about the products and the business.

Traditionally Used like historically. The idea is: "If *everyone* does it or says it, and always has, it must be so and therefore is okay."

Three levels down You want to build your group three levels deep. Refer to downline managers.

UPS shipping fee United Parcel Service does not ship free. You are charged by weight and zone. Call them for details.

Wholesale This is as cheap as you can get the product.

BIBLIOGRAPHY AND BOOKLIST

Abahsara, Michael, *The Healing Clay,* Swan House Publishing Co., P.O. Box 170, Brooklyn, NY 11223.

Andrecht, Venus, *The Outrageous Herb Lady or How to Make a Mint in Selling and Multi-Level Marketing,* Ransom Hill Press, P.O. Box 325, Ramona, CA 92065.

*Bamer, Donald R., Dr., *Applied Iridology and Herbology.*

Barlow, Max G., *From the Shepards Purse,* Spice West Co., Box 24, McCammon, ID 83250

*BiWorld, *Todays Herbs,* a newsletter.

Carter, Albert, *The Miracles of Rebound Exercise,* NIRH, 7416 212th S.W., Edmonds, WA 98020

Christopher, John, Dr., *Dr. Christopher's Natural Healing Newsletter,* Christopher Publications, P.O. Box 352, Provo, Utah 84601.

Failla, Don, *How to Build a Large Successful Multi-Level Marketing Organization,* Starr III Enterprises, P.O. Box 962, Gig Harbor, WA 98335.

*Foster, Rose Lewis, *Vitamin and Herb Almanac.*

*Griffin, LaDean, *Is Any Sick Among You, Eyes—Windows of The Body and Soul, Herbs to the Rescue, Herbs to the Rescue II, Hyper and Hypoglycemia, Cancer and the Parasite.*

*Heinerman, John, *Science of Herbal Medicine, The Treatment of Cancer With Herbs.*

*Jenks, Jim, *The Eyes Have It.*

*Jensen, Bernard, Dr., *Science and Practice of Iridology, Iridology Simplified.*

Jensen, Bernard, Dr., *Tissue Cleansing Through Bowel Management,* Dr. Bernard Jensen, Rt. 1 Box 52, Escondido, CA 92025.

*Malstrom, Stan, D.N.D., *Natural Treatment for Common Diseases; My Body, My Friend; Herbal Remedies II; Roots of Disease; Herbal Remedies for Common Diseases.*

Nature's Sunshine, *Sunshine Horizons,* a magazine, Nature's Sunshine Products, P.O. Box 1000, Spanish Fork, Utah 84660.

*Nebelkopf, Ethan, *The Herbal Connection, The New Herbalism.*

NHF, *Health Freedom News,* a magazine, National Health Federation, P.O. Box 688, Monrovia, CA 91016.

*Ritchason, Jack, *Little Herb Encyclopedia — Revised, Little Vitamin and Mineral Encyclopedia.*

Richason, Jack, *Iridology Correspondence Course,* Ritchason, 2425 Haley, Bakersfield, CA 93305.

Royal, Penny C., *Herbally Yours,* Sound Nutrition, 55 South 100 East, Orem, Utah 84057.

*Thompson, Robert, Dr., *A Handbook of Common Herbal Remedies.*

Tierra, Michael, *The Way of Herbs,* Unity Press, 235 Hoover Rd., Santa Cruz, CA 95065.

*Troyer, Samuel, Dr., *Holistic Herbal Healing,* Bi World Publishers, P.O. Box 1144, Orem, Utah 84057.

Walker, Norman W., *Colon Health,* O'Sullivan Woodside and Co., 2218 E. Magnolia, Phoenix, AZ 85034.

Weiss & Burnett, *Colon CLZ The Easy Way,* Weiss & Burnett, P.O. Box 479, Colfax, CA 95713.

Winter, Ruth, *A Consumer's Dictionary of Cosmetic Ingredients,* Crown Publishers, Inc., One Park Ave., New York, NY 10016.

*BiWorld Publishers, P.O. Box 1144, Orem, Utah 84057.

INDEX

SAMPLE NEWSLETTER CONTENTS

COMPETE WITH YOURSELF

The most effective way to make your herb business grow and astound you is to COMPETE WITH YOURSELF. I always set goals for ME. I never compare myself with what someone else is doing. Never. I decide I'll sell 10 bottles of ... in a week and I work like heck to do it. The next week it has to be 15. You might set a goal to find and teach one superior distributor everything you know. When you accomplish that you might set yourself a goal to find and teach two, then three, four and five, always doing better than you did yesterday or last month. Write your plans in soap on the bathroom mirror. Put your goal card on your desk, refrigerator or tape it and play the tape as you fall asleep. You may find you are pretty stiff competition. You will have plenty to do to keep besting yourself. You won't even notice how you stack up against another person. Best of all, you will become SUCCESSFUL.

****

SUSAN JENKINS is another one of us to watch. She moved to a strange area and just took over. She has her entire - HUGE - church involved in the herbs. We'll hear more about Susan! She's a future manager.

****

NEED HELP?

Keith (my husband, remember him?) is home for good. His specialty is helping you get your BUSINESS GOING AND BOOMING! He will sit down with you and work out a plan that suits your time, the type of life you have and people you come in contact with, your problems and your goals. He will help you set up a unique program to follow that will lead YOU to SUCCESS in the HERB BUSINESS. For an appointment, call Keith Smith,

****

VEGETABLE SEASONING BROTH AND SHAKER:

I put this on almost everything I eat. Regular people love it, too. It contains a healing pink salt that everyone can eat.

****

NEW PRODUCTS

WITH DONG QUOI: Hist., balances out the female hormones for menopausal, cramps, hysterectomy, puberty, sexual problems ... and DONG QUOI means "Compelled to Return to Normal Function." (We have both _____ and DONG QUOI separate, also.)

WITH ROYAL JELLY: Again, hist. balances out female hormones and ROYAL JELLY has a large reputation for making skin beautiful and is considered by many to be anti-aging, anti-wrinkling. (See info from many books on ROYAL JELLY.) Our company suggests it be used with our ——— products (the face cleaners, toners, creams and masque) to improve the skin. A lot of us use ———, (hair, skin and nails) too.

****

SALES AND MOTIVATION MEETINGS
Monday, 9:00 a.m. sharp!

These meetings start our week off with enthusiasm. We're learning sales techniques and end up getting so enthused, we do a whopping volume. Come try a class and see what you think. Every Monday, at 9:00, EXCEPT Potluck Monday. You missed a good one this week. I belly danced!

****

CLASSES

Potluck: May 3. Monday, 7 p.m. sharp. ON TIME DRAWING. Bring a dish. Iridology class.

Free Herb Education: Thurs., May 6 & 20. 7:30 p.m. Philosophical library, Escondido. Bring your distributors & retail people. Education is your key to a prosperous herb business.

Basic I & II Class: One class only this month. 7 p.m. sharp! Note time change. Our house. Learn how to *teach your people* MLM, the marketing plan, basic herb programs, introduction to all the products, slide presentations, etc. This is how we're now teaching our new people ... in one sitting. Come & learn & bring your people.

REMEMBER WE SHIP UPS TO YOUR DOOR

See you soon. *Love, Venus*

131

THE OUTRAGEOUS HERB LADY

WARNING!

Affluence May Be Hazardous To Your Wealth

THE BRIGHT SIDE

It's now eight years since I published the first edition of this book. A lot has happened in that time. I left that particular herb business and found a wonderful health and herb related multi-level company that's made me rather rich. I've pulled out of depressing sick-hood and near poverty to blooming good health and relative affluence, using the principles outlined in this book.

Unfortunately, this is not a book on making a marriage work, so I also went through a miserable divorce and lost almost everything I'd worked so hard for. That's why I ended up sickly and impoverished. I lost my home, my thriving herb business, my customers and even some of my friends. I had to start all over in order to support myself and my daughter Summer. I was even restrained by the divorce from selling herbs for several years. I had to find another multi-level business that I could believe in. Selling, and/or multi-level, are almost the only way a woman can make a decent living. I finally did find that good company and have become even more successful than I was the first time. Actually, wildly successful.

(Soon available, my latest book on how I built that business, *MLM MAGIC....How a Regular Person Can Build a Successful MLM Business from Scratch.* For further information, write: Ransom HIll Press, P.O. box 325, Ramona, CA 92065, or call 1-800-423-0620

If you're looking for a company, be cautious. You have to believe in the product you sell. No matter how good the company benefits may seem, if the product you're selling isn't worth the money, and the company isn't sound, it may go under. They often do. Check it out carefully, as it can mean the difference between prosperity and disaster for you.

Once you have become relatively successful with your chosen company and your paper work is under control, it's time for the other things you may want to do with your life.

Money is essential. We have trouble living without it. Only you can decide how much money is enough for you. If both husband and wife are working, you will have to be careful that what you bring in doesn't put you in a higher tax bracket, so that more goes out in taxes than if you'd made less.

I have reached a point in my life where I have money in the bank and can stop driving myself mercilessly to make more. I can take time to write more books, paint pictures and pursue my dreams. I can't afford to stop making money, but careful planning will give me time to enjoy what I make.

By following the principles laid down in this book, you may raise your income to dangerously high levels. It may be affected in the following ways:

TAXES.

I hadn't recovered from the shock of bringing in a sizeable monthly income when I was hit with the stunning news that the government could legally take away half of it. My immediate first step was to find a good tax person.

I found one, and the first thing she said after listening to my story was, "Get some write-off quick! Buy a house, a condo. Buy something that will allow you to write off the interest. Do you need some equipment for your business? Now is the time to get it."

I looked with envy at my downline. They didn't make the money I did, because they hadn't been in the business as long, but because they made less, they were able to spend more of their income on what they wanted to spend it on. After figuring out as much as I could about taxes, I passed the news onto them. After all, with persistence, they'd soon be where I was. The first thing I told them, and I'll tell you, is to find a knowledgeable tax person. Preferably someone who knows how to do multi-level! He/she will know all the appropriate deductions for your kind of work and he/she will also tell you that you're in the best business possible for write-offs. Write-offs such as the following:

HOME OFFICE:
If you work out of your home, you can write off :

     1) Part of your house payment
     2) Part of your utility bills .
     3) Part of your phone bill.

ENTERTAINMENT:

And for heaven's sake, if you have a party for your downline, you can
write off:

1) The cleaning bill
2) The food, and drinks
3) The good time, etc. It's almost like
being a congressman

SUPPLIES:

Also, by working out of your home, you'll find that
people traipsing in and out of your house all day, use lots of:

1) Toilet paper and paper towels.
2) They also drink water from your bottled water
3) Guzzle down sodas
4) Watch a number of product videos on your
VCR

These all figure into your tax deductions.

AUTO:

And your car! If you drive to a real job every day but
have to stop at the post office to get your business mail,
the whole trip is a tax write off.
Keep a little notebook in your car and record
your business mileage:

1) To where
2) When
3) For what purpose

PROMOTION:

Next, learn to be generous:

1) Buy your downline* little gifts. (At this writing
you can't deduct more than $25 per person.)
2) Take prospects and downline out to lunch and
dinner. Keep and write on every receipt:

a) The date
b) Place
c) Why you're there
d) Who you're with.

(*Downline. In a multi-level marketing business, your downline are the people who work under you. See glossary.)

OFFICE SUPPLIES

And remember office supplies. You need all kinds of things for your office. Maybe that beautiful set of Wedgewood china wouldn't fly with the IRS, but how about:

a) Tape
b) Notebooks
c) Pens
d) Paper, Staples, etc.—whatever it takes to run
your office
e) Office furniture.

Think about that comfortable office chair and neat lamp you've wanted for a long time?

KEEPING RECORDS:

Get a years supply of big manila envelopes and keep all receipts and records for your business in these, by month. January is full of January's business, for example.

Now that you have a few ideas about what MLM can do for your taxes, find and talk to that good tax person.

COMPUTERS ETC.

As for me, after I had talked to a tax person and was still reeling from the amount of money she said I'd owe, and that I should quickly buy something, my mother got hold of me.

"You need some write-off," she echoed. "You need a copier for your newsletters and the flyers you hand out at your meetings. How much money are you spending at the copy shop now? And more important, how much of your time does it take? Besides, you can write it off."

We had about a week left in that tax year. I panicked and mother flew into action.Two hours later she had me in a shop that sold copiers. Mr. Slick showed me a $6,000 re-built copier that did everything but spit in corners.Without any prodding I bought that massive mound of metal which was soon delivered to my quickly purchased townhouse by the sea. Well—for the next month or so, I spent more time with the copier repair man than I did with my family. I finally got the hang of running that, but Mother wasn't finished with me.

Before that last tax week was finished, she was saying, "You also need a computer to type in your newsletter, and to maintain your mailing list, and you need a printer to print them out." She sealed the deal by saying, "You can write them off."

I had utterly no interest in a computer and didn't know what a printer was, but I knew I had to spend the money or give it to the government...

I bought.

COMPUTERS ARE ALMOST MORE TAXING THAN TAXES

If I had thought mastering that copy machine was difficult, I didn't know what difficult was. The computer and I were not a good match. Fortunately, my daughter, Summer, seemed to catch on fairly quickly. She had, however, her moments of frustration. After several weeks of trying to teach me, she was ready to flunk me. One night, after an afternoon of computer generated turmoil and upset, the mailing list wouldn't print. We called my mother for help. I couldn't understand Mother's computer talk, so put a very tired, reluctant and petulant Summer on the phone and turned up the speaker phone. I watched and listened while Summer and Mother tussled with the apparently terminal condition of my mailing list. It appeared that it was gone forever, 400 names eaten by the humming plastic monster that now ruled my and Summer's lives. A half hour of controlled frustration went by. Mom would advise something. Summer would scowl and try it. Nothing would happen. Mother would suggest something else. Summer would try it. Nothing would happen. Computer books were whipped out and pages turned. Voices would rise. I'd try to be helpful by jiggling the plugs that led into the wall. Maybe they were loose?

It was much later now, and Summer had homework waiting. Not to mention her dinner, a bath and phone calls. Still Mother persisted, calling out one thing and another which Summer dutifully tried. Summer began to get *That Look* on her face. I know *That Look*. It means there's going to be an explosion of rare but startling proportions.

"That's enough for tonight," I said to Summer.

"Mom," I called out over the speaker, "We have to hang up, now. I've lost my entire business, of course, because my mailing list is gone, and now we'll starve, but... Summer, hang up the phone."

"Good night, Grandma," Summer said, as she put the phone in it's cradle. Then, she looked at me.

I was about to say, "You have to hit the speaker button. Grandma's still on the line." But, I didn't have a chance.

Summer rose up out of her chair as if jerked by a thousand strings. She flailed her arms through the air and went strictly berserk, screaming obscenities about computers in general and mine in particular.

"Summer, Summer..." I soothed, pointing at the phone, "Grandma's still on the..."

"What? What?" Grandma piped from the other edge of the county. "What? What?"

Summer paled, flopped back in her chair and looked at me, startled, contrite and embarrassed. "Oh Grandma," she said meekly. "I'm so sorry." She hung her head.

"That's O.K., Summer, "Mom soothed. "I have a computer, too, you know."

We did eventually find and get that mailing list printed, but I realized that Summer had her own busy life and it didn't include teaching a computer illiterate. I was going to have to learn to use that computer myself. I signed up for a computer class. There were two sessions. I took the first session and came home even more confused than I'd been before. I was so confused I didn't go to the second session, but got the book out, kept Summer home to help me, and the phone to mother close by. It wasn't easy, but I finally learned to type in my newsletter and print out my mailing list. And if I can do it, I know you can, too.

If you have reached this point of affluence, I would like to suggest that before you buy your computer, either have someone close by who knows how to run it, or carefully check out the computer stores near you. You are looking for a store with at least one knowledgeable employee who will willingly answer your questions at any time you need help. You may have to pay extra for this service, but it's also deductible.

First, though, decide if you really need a computer. It's not good business to buy something you don't need and won't use just because you can write it off.

DO YOU REALLY NEED A COMPUTER?

You need a computer if:

- Your typewriter can't keep up with your paper work
- You can't find names and addresses you need when you need them
- The newsletter should go out next week and all your information is on little scraps of paper somewhere
- Your mailing list is huge and growing
- Your mailing list is so large you have a bulk mail permit and have to count, sort, bundle and bag by zip code
- You spend too much time on your bookkeeping

You don't need a computer if:

- You're an excellent typist and it's easy for you to get your letters out on time and looking good
- Your mailing list is less than 200 names and easy to maintain
- You are well-organized
- You can keep your bank book balanced with little trouble
- You can get help when you need it.

Computers are expensive, time-consuming, and frustrating, to learn. It might be cheaper and easier for you to hire help when you need it. (Also deductible.) This is a decision only you can make.

ACCOUNTING

Once you've entered the magic world of computers, you can't stop with a word processing and mailing list program, (or so my mother says). Mom says, "With all this business coming in, you will need an accounting, or bookkeeping, system to keep track of it."

I don't always listen to my mother, so, I'm still doing my book-keeping by hand and when I look at what my mother has been going through in order to put her accounting program in place, I don't know if I have the courage to change. She has a program called *DacEasy©*.

"It's not easy," she says. I see her spending almost a third of her time, and reams of paper, doing her accounting. She has another program for my father's Real Estate business called *Quicken©*. She loves it. It's simple, (she says) and saves time and agony at the end of the year when she has to get her records together for the accountant She likes it so well that when she finishes struggling with *DacEasy©*, she puts all her information into *Quicken©* and uses that for her book business, too.

A FEW WORDS FROM MOTHER

If your business is a simple one with only one product to sell, and you have no employees, you don't really need a computer. If you already have a computer, then putting a simple pro-gram, like *Quicken©* on it will save you time, keep good records, and ensure correct calculations. *Quiken©* is a simple accounting program that is relatively inexpensive.There are versions for the IBM and the Macintosh©. Another similar one, for the Macintosh, is *MacMoney©*. It won't keep track of inventory, or print out invoices, or statements, but will write checks, reconcile your bank statement and print out tax-return reports. If your business is simple, Quicken© is a program you can handle yourself.

1. Type the information into *Quicken©*, unless you can find something you like better
Every check you write is recorded on the computer You assign it to a category, which you have set up. Categories like: Advertising, Cost of product, Utilities, gas etc. Whatever you have to keep track of for your taxes. At tax time it's all in the

computer waiting to be printed out.

2.Each time you make a deposit, break your income down. I break mine down like this:
a) taxable
b) non-taxable
c) out of state
d) shipping costs
e) credit
f) refunds

Your items may differ from mine, but you will have a record of your income at tax time.

It is possible to get *Shareware*, or *Public Domain* software that will do the invoices, and labels. The stores that sell this software usually advertise in little give–away magazines carried by computer stores, bookstores and sometimes grocery stores. There are more of these programs for the IBM than the Macintosh. Again, these programs are very inexpensive but come without much in the way of instruction, so be sure you have someone to turn to for help in using them. If it's a *Shareware* program and you like and use the program, you're supposed to send money to the person who designed it. You will then be registered for updates and get some documentation (a book of instructions). *Public Domain* software is free.

Whether you use a computer or not, you need to know how much money you have in the bank. The best way to do that is to keep your checkbook balanced. Venus told me she doesn't reconcile her checkbook each month, she's too busy making money. She figures if she keeps putting in as much as she can, and taking out as little as possible, she won't need to worry. O.K. for Venus maybe, dangerous for the rest of us.

Venus is a saver. We could all learn from her. No matter how much money you have coming in now, don't spend all of it. Save as much as you can. Life is a roller coaster. What goes up can come crashing down.

BALANCE YOUR CHECKBOOK WITH OR WITH-OUT A COMPUTER   (Venus, I hope you read this.)

Balancing a checkbook doesn't seem difficult to me now, but when I first got married, I didn't know how to write a check, let alone balance a checkbook. My husband did all the book-keeping and check writing. But, once a month, at check writing time, he would sink into a black hole of depression. Watching all that money go out for the necessities of life was almost more than he could bear. His depressions were more than I could bear. It was a long slow struggle to take over the family/business bookkeeping and get it to always balance. It took years, but I did it. Learning to balance my checkbook was agony. It's really simple and all the instructions are on your bank statement. I didn't read them, of course.

I didn't learn to balance my checkbook until our CPA wrote out these step-by-step instructions for me.
If you have no trouble with your checkbook, skip this section.

• Open your bank statement. Look at the list of checks on the front of the statement. (Where it says CHECKS/OTHER DEBITS.) If they are listed by check number, put the checks in numerical order. If they're listed some other way, go through the checks as they are. In either case:

• Mark off each check, on the statement, as you come to it. You need to know that all the checks are there. The bank rarely makes mistakes, but it has happened. I've had the bank leave a few cents off of a check in their computer, and I've wasted a lot of time trying to find *my* mistake. Look at the bottom right hand corner of the check. The amount of the check entered in their computer will be printed there. If all the checks are there and the amounts are correct:

• Sort your checks by number, if you haven't already done this, then:

• Check off the numbered checks in your checkbook (or your computer). Put a √ or an X next to each.

• Check off your deposits the same way

• Record in your checkbook any credits or withdrawals, such as service charges, that show up on your statement

• Turn your bank statement over. On the back, under STEP ONE, list all your outstanding checks. (The ones that didn't get a check mark in your checkbook). Add them up. Record the total

• Note on the front of your statement, under SUMMARY, the amount that follows STATEMENT BALANCE ON (whatever date)

• Turn your statement over again and record the statement Balance on line number 1. The line that asks for: THIS STATEMENT'S BALANCE

• If you have deposits listed in your checkbook that don't appear on your statement, add them to your statement balance and enter the amount where it says SUBTOTAL

• Enter the total of your outstanding checks where it says SUBTRACT CHECKS/OTHER DEBITS NOT LISTED IN THIS STATEMENT and subtract it from the SUBTOTAL, or from THIS STATEMENT'S BALANCE if there is no SUBTOTAL.

This amount, YOUR CURRENT CHECKBOOK BALANCE, should agree with your checkbook. If you haven't added that up, do so. The advantage of a computer is that it's faster and it always computes correctly."

Thanks, Mom. To put you at ease (or cause you to worry more).I never figure my interest either, of course, so I always hope I'm money ahead!"

OUR FINANCIAL FUTURE

At the same time my tax lady said I needed to immediately spend money to save some, she also told me I needed to save some in order not to have to spend it or give it to the government. (Pretty soon you realize *Money and Taxes* are a game that people play to keep themselves occupied. I personally find it a stupid game, but when you have money you're automatically thrown into the ring and to get out alive, you have to learn the rules. *Fast!*)

To "help" me, I engaged the services of a financial advisor. With that, I experienced a near miss, almost landing myself in a pension plan that would cause me to always drop in large sums yearly, and have a whopping yearly management fee of close to $1,000. Somehow a fund employee at my bank got wind of the money I was thinking of tossing and tried to get me to enroll in a plan through him. There ensued quite an argument between him and the man who ran the pension plan, each accusing the other of saying whatever was necessary to get my account. So I called a stockbroker for advice and, of course, then had him after me with his plans. After several months of this uproar along with my leg dragging, my advisor decided I was right, that this particular pension plan wasn't a good deal for me.

I opened a SEP/IRA* account and at the last possible moment, tossed the necessary money into it.The necessary money was the most I was allowed tuck away, that I would have had to give to Uncle Sam, if I hadn't had a SEP/IRA. SEP/IRA stands for *Simplified Employees Pension Plan*. A retirement plan for people who have MLMs, or are self-employed. This allows us to save money for our old age, because no employer has a plan for us.By the time I got through buying equipment to save taxes, paying taxes, pouring money into the SEP/IRA and paying my tax lady, I was flat out of money. My less affluent friends had more.

SEP/IRA allows allows a yearly investment of either 15%, of what you earn or $30,000, whichever is less. A plain IRA will only allow you to put $2000 into your pension plan yearly no matter how much you earn. If you make a lot of money, you need the SEP/IRA.

ORDER BLANK

RANSOM HILL PRESS BOOKS
A Family Publishing Company

_____ MLM Magic, V. Andrecht .... 16.95 _____

_____ MLM Magic (in Spanish), V. Andrecht .... 18.95 _____

_____ The Herb Lady's Notebook, V. Andrecht ...... 16.95 _____

_____ The Outrageous Herb Lady, V. Andrecht ...... 12.95 _____

_____ Tape #1 – Money Out of Control, V. Andrecht

(Audio Tape & Booklet) .... 9.95 _____

_____ "Dear Venus" Letters .... 5.95 _____

_____ Tea Cup Tales, M. McWhorter *(Venus's mother)* .. 5.95 _____

_____ Poems That Tell Me Who I Am, M. McWhorter .. 4.95 _____

_____ Autumn Leaves, M. McWhorter .... 4.95 _____

_____ Drift On The River, P. Rozelle *(Venus's aunt)* ...... 9.95 _____

Make checks payable to:
Ransom Hill Press
P.O. Box 325, Ramona, CA 92065-0325

California residents, add appropriate state sales tax.
Shipping: $2.00 for first book, $.50 each additional book.
Priority Mail, $3.50 1st book, $.50 each additional book.
Out of country, please call. COD, add $4.50 to shipping cost.

_____ Payment enclosed. Charge my: _____ MasterCard _____Visa

Card # _____

Expiration date:_____ Phone ( ) _____

Name: _____

Address: _____

City: _____ State:_____ Zip:_____

Visa or MasterCard
1-800-423-0620
US & Canada
(619) 789-0620
out of U.S.
FAX 619-789-1582

DISCOUNT SCHEDULE
Mix & Match

1 Item	0%
2 – 3	10%
4 – 5	20%
6 – 10	25%
11 – Up	30%

Call for Volume Discount!

Prices subject to change without notice.